LOUISVILLE
ARCHITECTURAL
TOURS

19TH CENTURY GEMS

lucy from
Lu
C'mas '08

Lisa Westmoreland-Doherty

4880 Lower Valley Road · Atglen, Pennsylvania 19310

Designed by Stephanie Daugherty
Type set in Trajen Pro/NewBskvll BT/
Humanist521 BT

ISBN: 978-0-7643-3038-4
Printed in China

Schiffer Books are available at special discounts for bulk purchases for sales promotions or premiums. Special editions, including personalized covers, corporate imprints, and excerpts can be created in large quantities for special needs. For more information contact the publisher:

Published by Schiffer Publishing Ltd.
4880 Lower Valley Road
Atglen, PA 19310
Phone: (610) 593-1777;
Fax: (610) 593-2002
E-mail: Info@schifferbooks.com

For the largest selection of fine reference books on this and related subjects, please visit our web site at:
www.schifferbooks.com

We are always looking for people to write books on new and related subjects. If you have an idea for a book please contact us at the above address.

This book may be purchased from the publisher. Include $5.00 for shipping. Please try your bookstore first. You may write for a free catalog.

In Europe, Schiffer books are distributed by

Bushwood Books
6 Marksbury Ave.
Kew Gardens
Surrey TW9 4JF England
Phone: 44 (0) 20 8392-8585
Fax: 44 (0) 20 8392-9876
E-mail: info@bushwoodbooks.co.uk
Website: **www.bushwoodbooks.co.uk**

Free postage in the U.K., Europe; air mail at cost.

CONTENTS

GLOSSARY

"WHAT AM I SEEING?"

Vocabulary is an important aspect of the study of architecture. Without knowing the vocabulary of a particular art form, it is difficult to identify specific features and describe what one is seeing. In classical education, the study of architecture was a vital part of the Humanities and was often seen as the cornerstone upon which other disciplines were based. However, through the years, the perception of architecture has changed. While it may have been viewed in ancient times as a more functional form of artistry, in modern times the study of architecture as an art form is usually reserved for those who study its history in Humanities or classes in design. Most people today value buildings and homes for the purpose they serve, often overlooking the subtle elements that make statements about our time and culture. Sculptures and paintings please the eye. They have value on multiple cultural levels, sometimes marking a page in history or reflecting the values and traditions of specific cultures. Architecture has a very tangible purpose. Creation of buildings – homes, offices, high-rise apartments, churches, cathedrals, and schools – is an act of will, an act of creation that satisfies a particular social necessity. But it also satisfies the need for the artist to create. There is a specific purpose in designing and constructing buildings. They *house* things. They keep things safe. They cover and inform. Buildings take on real purpose in the lives of human beings and assist them in their daily lives. The importance of homes, churches, and buildings cannot be underestimated and it's with this in mind that I begin this book with a series of words that will assist you in your understanding of key terms and concepts listed within. Additionally, they might help us all discover and uncover these elements of architecture in the buildings around Louisville, and, perhaps, in your own city as well. It is my hope that you come away from this book with a new and improved vision of the importance of the homes in your area and a renewed – or new – desire to preserve the historical homes and architectural heritage of the city in which you live.

Battlements: These specific architectural designs are also called *crenellations* and are portions of a wall that are cut away, reminding one of the defensive wall around the top portion of a castle or fort. Originally, this was used so that those who were shooting arrows or firing at an enemy would have a place to discharge their ammunition, while remaining relatively safe from attackers.

Balustrade: A porch that is comprised of a railing with balusters, which are smaller rails that support the top of the railing.

Capital: The top part of the column that exists as decoration or often for the support of the triangular shaped pediment. The three common types of capital are the Doric, Ionic, and Corinthian.

Column: A pillar that exists for support or decoration. There are three basic parts: the base or bottom, the shaft or middle, and the capital or top decorative portion.

Cornices: The word cornice comes from the Italian word that means "ledge." A cornice ornamentally crowns the top of a building. The purpose is functional, as it is meant to keep rainwater off of a building's walls.

Cupola/Cuppola: Not depending on the spelling (I have seen it spelled both ways) a cupola is the structure that sits on top of the roof and will often have a weather vane. Sometimes the cupola is dome shaped, hence the name. It was supposed to originally resemble a small cup that was turned upside down. However, depending on the era and what was popular at the time, the cupola can be square or quadrilateral. It is often a great source of natural light for the inside of a building. Most that I have seen are decorative or ornamental only.

Eaves: Eaves are the part of the roof that overhangs the edges. Depending on the architectural style, you will find moldings, dentils, or other ornamentation under the eaves. The original function was to provide protection from the weather. Because the eave is underneath the edge of the roof, there is an amount of protection for where the wall and roof meet.

Finial: There is not much of a true function, per se, to a finial, other than pretty ornamentation. These decorative projections that sit atop a spire or a pinnacle draw attention upward and are great additions to church spires, where the eye and concentration are ever drawn toward God.

Foil: The leaf-like, or lobe of a curve or an arch, the foil is often found in windows of churches, especially Gothic Revival style, and the prefix will indicate how many lobes there are in the foil. For instance, some windows have a quatrefoil, which is a decorative four-lobed structure, while others have a trefoil, which would have three lobes.

Gable: A triangular shaped roof that allows the rain and snow to fall off easily.

Gingerbread: The heavy ornamentation on the porches and trim of a home or building. This term is usually used to describe the Victorian homes of the late 1800s. The gingerbread designs are unique to the individual structure and vary according to what was popular in the area at a particular time, but the term itself is very generic and can be used to describe any number of ornamental embellishments on a Victorian building.

Gothic Arch: A pointed arch that has equal radii. This type of arch differs from a traditional rounded arch in that the center is pointed and not round. The traditional Gothic arch is popular for windows in cathedrals and in molded doorways or windows. While arches are popular, in my opinion, the Gothic arch is one of the most elegant arch forms.

Hood Mold or Hooded Molding: The area above a door or a window that is used to throw off the rain. It may give the door or window a "recessed" look and may be heavily ornamented depending on the style of the home or building.

Turret: A small tower that projects from the side of a building. The turret is usually a part of the larger structure and I have heard them referred to on some occasions as a "widow's tower." This could be in part due to the myth that widows would look out the window at what was going on in the world around them. Since the mourning phase for a woman after she lost a husband would be a year, she would often stay in until the mourning time was over. A turret is a structure that resembles a small rounded tower and usually does not sit on the ground, but is above it.

INTRODUCTION

"VISIONS AND REVISIONS"

The room was round and the house smelled of candy and talcum powder. The window faced out toward the street and the little seat in front of it was covered with a pink floral cushion that had large buttons on it. I ran my small eight-year-old fingers over it and marveled at how a room could be round. Inside that home it felt like I did when I said the word *lady* and meant it. While the soft lamp glowed, I looked around and saw the staircase, completely made of wood, leading, I was certain, to a room filled with pink and white furnishings, heavy silver mirrors, and lamps that wore frilly little skirts around the base of the shade, as if they were demurely trying to hide what was underneath. The entire house smelled of tiny cookies and apple cider. All my life I had passed that house, still located on Frankfort Avenue, and dreamed of going inside. I remember being so thankful that Halloween gave me the chance to step inside while the lady of the house gathered my candy and cookies, but more than that I remembered thinking, "Someday, my house will be just like this." That night I fell head over heels in love with Victorian homes and it has been a life-long passion that has not diminished with the passage of time. Eagerly I anticipated exploring each of the districts in the city, examining why certain ethnic groups migrated to one area over another. I was anxious to discover why my family came from Germantown, while other families settled in the

A broad view and a close up of homes on Fourth Avenue.

Highlands. How did immigrants affect the wealth of an area? Why were some homes built in one style and in other areas, a completely different style? I expected to find a plethora of information and people beating down my door to share their family stories. However, what I found disheartened me. Many of the stories and local lore regarding the founders of our city have been lost to the ages because families did not primarily write down their tales. They were passed down orally from generation to generation and unless you were the *griot*, or story-keeper, of your family, chances are good that the tales were lost forever. The *griot* was usually a woman, an old auntie or grandmother, who would know the exact date when everyone was born and everyone died. She could tell you why your family lived where they did and all the juicy stories about everyone else in the area. This figure was especially prevalent in the African American communities, since prior to the Civil War, family history was most commonly passed down orally. The figure of the griot continues to be important, but it's no longer limited to the African American community. There is usually one person who takes over the preservation of the stories and history in any family. If one is lucky, sometimes there are several from various branches to share the responsibility. When I started thinking about preserving history and the importance of story-telling in our community, this book took a different direction. I went from simply wanting to write a book about homes and buildings to truly desiring a place in the preservation of my community and the stories that make it beautiful and special. In the past few years, there has been a renewed interest in preserving some of the more historic districts such as Fourth Street and Downtown Louisville; but for those districts that have primarily gone unnoticed due to increasing poverty and disrepair there are precious few people who care enough to preserve the buildings or history. Groups like the Portland Historical Society have made a tremendous difference in the amount of pride the local residents take in their district. Interest in the historical preservation of the buildings in the Portland district has really taken off in recent months, and thanks to these groups buildings from the 1700s are no longer resigned to falling into the dust of the ages and eventual destruction.

The buildings in Louisville are among some of the most beautiful I have seen in North America. The looming Victorian mansions that I dreamed about owning one day used to be ritualistic stopping points on my bicycle rides around the Frankfort Avenue area and I felt a certain kinship with these places. These buildings had a life of their own, existing long before I ever came onto the scene. These were the structures in our community that had lasted through the years. These were the structures that had withstood the harshest of elements and the ravages of time and were, to me, bastions of durability that epitomized the eternal struggle that we as humans face as we come to terms with our own impermanence. However, it is often those things that do not last that we cling to most desperately.

I have always been of the opinion that there are primarily two types of people in the world. There are those who love the Beatles and those

who love the Rolling Stones. There are those who love oatmeal and those who love cream of wheat. There are those who value the historic building or home and what it brings to the community as a whole, and then there are those who see a great place where a parking lot could go — once the building was torn down, that is. I have not completed my theory about which group falls where, as I am still working on some of the discrepancies, but I think you can get the general idea. In addition to being a Beatles kind of gal, it just so happens that I also love anything that holds the possibility of a good story—as stories are the substance that holds our society together. Stories are the thread that binds together the past and present, creating the colorful and interesting communities that I know so well.

I knew early on that I was destined to be one of those people who horded all kinds of worthless artifacts and heirlooms that I could one day share with others, telling the stories and behind-the-scenes events as if I were a true primary source. I believed I had a treasure trove of goodies, simply because I knew the stories behind them and the stories were what made them valuable to me. The trinkets that my grandmothers passed down to me and that my mother has given me through the years became more than just objects. They were symbols of strength and endurance. The worn out wedding rings became more than just a little bit of gold; they were lasting, tangible object lessons that reflected the values and the lives of those who treasured them and kept them safe all through the years. Homes and buildings are different than Granny Betty's turn-of-the-century baby shoes or Poppy Rudolph's tiny New Testament that he carried into World War I when he was stationed in Normandy. Buildings are places where lives are changed forever based on what happens inside them. Homes hold families together and the structures become more than mere brick and stone or wood. Office buildings hold contracts, as well as the lives and futures of those who work there. Whether it is a home, a church, or an office building, the structures often take on aspects of the lives that are lived within and become an extension of the personalities of the people who make the buildings an important part of their lives. By looking at the architecture and construction of a building, one can often tell a lot about the time, place, and the lives of the homeowners from the very first inhabitants to the very latest. Were those who lived there nouveau riche, looking to find a place where they could become the New American aristocracy? Were they laborers who just wanted to make a life for their families or start over anew in a place where they felt like they had a fighting chance at moving up the social ladder? The places examined in this book shed a little

light on the form and function of the structures that were built when our city was still in its infancy; and, in the process, how these things have helped the buildings survive well into the twenty-first century. It is with preservation in mind that I have undertaken this project. I hoped to capture bits and pieces of the history of the specific districts of the city, but more than that, I hoped to capture the humanity that surrounds these buildings and that continue to touch our lives throughout the years.

In 1974 I was only four years old, but I can still remember when the most devastating tornado in Louisville's history struck our small community. The neighborhoods were decimated, with many of the homes leveled to the ground. I walked with my parents, holding their hands, and watching as the people we called our friends stared at the rubble and boards that used to be the stately houses they called home. We all stood there speechless, as if witnessing death itself, and simply could not find words conciliatory enough to even utter to each other. When disaster strikes, often times the best we can do for each other is to be present and silent. Words like "I'm sorry" just minimize the catastrophe. This one singularly destructive force of nature brought some of the most historic homes in the city to the ground and preservationists came in droves to save our neighborhoods. Some could be saved or salvaged and others could not, as human craftsmanship can only go so far in what it constructs. Yet, what does manage to withstand the natural wear and tear of time is often treasured for its remarkable durability and will often signify the work of great architectural geniuses, such as the pyramids or the great columns of ancient Greece. But the homes in Louisville that were affected by the 1974 tornado were not constructed of marble and limestone, and many were unable to hold up against the ravages of severe weather and the flooding that is still quite common in some areas of the city. They fell into disrepair over the years and were lost. When a structure is lost due to natural disaster, it's torn down and a great bare spot on a plot of grass is all that will remain. People will, as they drive or walk by, comment to their children, "That is where such and such used to be before the flood," or something similar. However, there are many buildings that defied the odds and have lasted despite the disasters. Through the care of those in the community and the refusal to let the tornado destroy the spirit of those living there, most of the homes and buildings were saved and continue to be places of interest today.

In one of my graduate classes at the University of Louisville, we were given an assignment to take a walking tour of Old Louisville, which is comprised mostly of Third and Fourth Streets, and Belgravia Court. I hesitate to call the structures and buildings "homes" even though that was their original purpose. Today, many of them function as office buildings or apartment complexes, but it is easily discernable that the intent was for them to house single, affluent families in a very well-to-do neighborhood. The class I took focused on architecture, as

well as other areas of the Humanities, but it was the first time in my life that I realized that there were others like me who loved the buildings and our city's history as much as I did. Until that class, when I heard others talking about the beauty and elegance of the buildings that surrounded us, I never understood how important architecture was to the study of the Humanities. I always assumed that Humanities was the study of art, literature, and dance. I never considered buildings to be "art" even though I knew that I loved what I saw and was fiercely connected to our city. But, could architecture really be an expression of an artistic soul? As I walked through downtown Louisville on that cold November evening, researching the buildings that were required for the class, I began to wonder about the differences among the buildings. Why were some buildings structured in one way and another in a completely different form? I longed for more information as I started to understand that sometimes buildings are constructed out of necessity and whatever service they are providing to the public tends to be the guiding factor as to how they are constructed. Other times, buildings are adorned, fabricated, and fashioned in ways that make a statement about the owners of the homes, their personal values, and, quite by chance, the time periods when they were built. The vision and artistry of the architect and designer works together today in the same way it did at the turn of each century. Much like the work of a sculptor, the block of stone or planks of wood reflect the vision, creativity, and talent of people who see past the stone and mortar. Louisville has a rich assortment of structures including office buildings, private residences, beds and breakfasts, historic homes, and many other, less auspicious, yet nonetheless interesting dwellings. It is with great pride in my city and the buildings that reflect our cultural heritage and creative spirit that I begin my journey into the exploration of the architecture of Louisville.

"Our Place in History"

I find it extremely difficult to understand the history of an area if I am faced with dates and places, but have no historical context with which to understand them. For me, it's as if the location or event exists in a vacuum. In other words, it is very hard for me to understand the date "1792," which marks when Kentucky officially joined the Union of the United States, if I do not know that at that time George Washington was President. I cannot understand the importance of a building constructed in "1853" if I do not understand that our country was fewer than ten years away from Civil War and that Kentucky was trying to decide where it stood on the issue of slavery. Knowing historic dates helps us place Louisville's architecture within a framework of events. It's with this in mind that I have arranged a timeline of events that may help you, the reader, to have a framework for the actual construction of the buildings.

TIMELINE

1769: Daniel Boone explores the Kentucky wilderness; founds Boonesboro.
1776: Independence is declared from England and the Revolutionary War begins.
1778: George Rogers Clark founds Louisville, which is named for King Louis XVI of France.
1783: Peace Treaty finally ends the Revolutionary War.
1784: Benjamin Franklin invents bi-focal glasses.
1785: Springfield, the home of future President, Zachary Taylor, is constructed.
1788: The United States Constitution is ratified.
1789: The Bill of Rights is adopted in the United States.
   • The French Revolution begins, ending France's monarchy.
1790: Locust Grove is founded by the Clark and Croghan families.
1791: The Bill of Rights is finally put into effect.
1792: The Commonwealth of Kentucky officially splits from Virginia and is accepted into the Union.
1793: Eli Whitney invents the "Cotton Gin," (short for cotton engine). This invention increased cotton production and the need for more slaves in the Southern states.
   • Louis XVI and Marie Antoinette are executed.
1799: Napoleon becomes Consul.
1801: Thomas Jefferson takes office as President.
1803: Lewis and Clark, along with the Corps of Discovery, begin an expedition to the Pacific Ocean.
1804: Napoleon becomes Emperor of France.
1811: Portland, Louisville, is established.
1812: The War of 1812 – America fights again with Britain.
1815: The Squire Jacob Earick house is constructed.
1830: Indian Removal Act (Trail of Tears) is passed.
1831: Presentation Academy is founded by Mother Spalding.
1839: Notre Dame du Port is established.
1845: The Portland Marine Hospital is established.
1846: The Mexican War begins.
1848: Walnut Street Baptist Church is erected.
1850: The Thomas Edison House is built.
1852: *Uncle Tom's Cabin*, by Harriet Beecher Stowe, is published, sparking outrage against slavery.
1853: Heigold House is completed and the Inn at Woodhaven is constructed.
1855: "Know Nothing" riots of Butchertown claims lives and create mayhem.
1861-1865: The American Civil War is fought.
1865: Abraham Lincoln is assassinated by John Wilkes Booth at Ford's Theatre.
1869: Transcontinental Railroad is built.

1871: The Wesley House is constructed.

1874: The Women's Christian Temperance Movement is founded.

1878: The Women's Suffrage amendment is introduced to Congress, but isn't ratified until 1920.

1876: St. Joseph's Cathedral is constructed.

1879: Thomas Edison invents the incandescent light bulb.

1883: The Southern Exposition in Louisville highlights Thomas Edison's new invention.

1891: The "Pink Palace" is built, and the Merriwether House is constructed.

1892: The Condrad-Caldwell House is constructed.

1895: St. Mark's Episcopal Church is built.

1900: Lampton Baptist Church is built.

1905: Ferguson Mansion is completed; Louisville Free Public Library is established.

AN OVERVIEW

Kentucky existed as a place for settlers and farmers long before it was officially recognized in 1792. It might also be noted that the European settlers who had come from Virginia into Kentucky were not the first people to set foot on Kentucky soil. Anyone who ever watched Fess Parker play the part of Daniel Boone knows that long before he explored the vast wilderness, there were people here – nations of people – who had lived, farmed, and hunted on this land. Original settlers would have been forced to share the Kentucky land with the Native American groups that were indigenous to the region. Some historians would say that there are likely four or five Native American nations that claim Kentucky and its land as their home. One should note that Native American peoples are no longer called "Indians" or "tribes" as the names suggest savage, uncivilized clan, which these nations most definitely were not. The nations had their own system of government, beliefs, customs, and unique social structure, which would imply that they were an advanced civilization by any standard. Yet, it is only with our perspective as an enlightened society that we can make these observations. The European settlers did not have this worldview and the Cherokee, Shawnee, Yucci, Chicksaw, as well as other tribes, were eventually ousted from their lands. During the Presidency of Andrew Jackson, many Native Americans were forced from their homes and hunting grounds. New legislation combined with the demand for more land and greater control of the western territories, making it necessary to reduce the risk of invasion and uprising from the Native Americans. Jackson passed the "Indian Removal Act," forcing all Native Americans to move out west and putting them on smaller tracts of land called Reservations. This would come to be known as the infamous "Trail of Tears" due to the sadness and death that followed the Cherokee on their way out west. Although the nations were removed, history cannot erase their presence in Kentucky, for many places in Louisville still bear the names of the peoples who inhabited this area. Names such as Algonquin Parkway, Iroquois Shopping Center, and Cherokee Park are all so familiar to those who live here that we do not often stop to think about those for who the areas are named. It's interesting that there are so many different nations or tribes represented in Louisville because boundaries would have been an issue for those who inhabited the area. The Algonquin Parkway is located quite near to Iroquois Manor, but that does not mean that both nations co-existed in the same area at the same time. It is plausible that this is just a way to pay tribute to the nations that lived in Kentucky, but does not indicate that they lived in the actual area of the mall or parkway. Territorial disputes were common among the Native Americans, but when the white settlers came into their land, they brought with them death and destruction unlike anything the nations had seen before.

Long before we were legitimately accepted into the Union of the United States, there were many families who called this area home. Families such as mine, who have been here for more than ten generations, know that we were once part of the Virginia Territories and Kentucky was a tremendous draw for those wanting to farm. The land closely resembles that of Virginia and is excellent for growing crops such as corn and tobacco. The rich, fertile soil was an agriculturalist's dream and Kentucky continues to be a leading producer of tobacco in the United States as a result. Many families came, settling into what is now known as the Fayette County area, namely Lexington and the surrounding cities. They began homesteading and farming the land, setting up businesses and putting down roots. The land dictates to the farmer what it will allow to be grown in its soil and, while some areas of Kentucky are extremely conducive for cultivating and harvesting crops, other areas are not quite as good. Farmland rolls, deepening into a rich, deep green in the summer time, while other areas remain fields of clay dirt. As with most areas of the country, people will farm where they can, and when they cannot, they will find other ways of making a living or thriving off the natural resources of the area. For this reason, cities located near the river became central locations for those wishing to trade up and down the Ohio River. The Ohio River drew many people to its banks, as it gave opportunities for trading wares. Once a stop for slave traders, Louisville still bears a sad memorial to those who once stood on the auction block, sold like animals to those who enslaved them. There is a marker that reminds those who visit it that such tragedy and injustice was once part of our history and must never be forgotten, lest such things happen again. However, there were also those who had goods and services to trade or sell ad many people found the Louisville area a fantastic place to start a new and hopefully prosperous life. People traveled up and down the River, getting off to eat, drink, change boats, or rest. Sailors would get off and rest for a bit while passengers might choose to stay and settle down with relatives that lived in the area. What cannot be denied is that out of necessity, the American spirit of enterprise and entrepreneurialism thrives.

When looking at the city of Louisville and its history, one family name that cannot be overlooked is the Clark family. The ties that the Clarks have to Kentucky are inextricably linked with the history of a prospering new nation, but George Rogers Clark would find that even war heroes have to deal with universal human difficulties and addictions. Even though the family was old and well respected, it did not exempt them from tragedy.

If the surname "Clark" sounds familiar to you, it could be that you are remembering your middle school history. After all, William Clark was a man who was well known throughout the country and many of the greatest men of the time were proud to call him friend. William Clark had a companion who would also play an integral part in the settling and exploration of the blossoming new nation. The other half of the dynamic duo was Meriwether Lewis, a man Clark recommended personally to Thomas Jefferson when Jefferson commissioned him and, subsequently, Lewis to undertake the task of cataloging the territory. Most people mistakenly assume that Clark's and Lewis's only job was to find out if there was a way to get to the Pacific Ocean. What is often overlooked are the great discoveries made along the journey. The pair, with their brilliant guide Sacagewea, who also acted as a translator, catalogued plants, trees and animals across the previously unexplored territory. Their diaries hold a wealth of information that was an invaluable resource to our country. They and the other members of what was called the "Corps of Discovery" kept journal entries and pictures of the plants and wildlife they encountered. Louisville figures into the lives of the prominent explorers and into this segment of history in a very simple and practical way. William Clark's sister, Lucy, was married to a man who lived on a lovely estate called Locust Grove. The sister, fond of her brother and his compatriot, Mr. Lewis, would offer them a place to stay and rest when they traveled through the area. Additionally, Lucy would become the sole caregiver for their older brother, George Rogers Clark, when alcoholism and years of hard living finally caught up with him. She cared for him until he died, which is a testament to the strength and loyalty the Clark family had for one another. Even in this most respectable of historic families there are skeletons that cannot be hidden and that shed light on why people end up where they do. General George Rogers Clark was not a man who was unfamiliar to the founding fathers of our country. He was intimately acquainted with both Thomas Jefferson and Governor Patrick Henry to name just two. Historians credit General Clark as being the founder of the city of Louisville somewhere around the year 1778 after he had been entrusted with what was then known as "Kentucky County." General Clark had previously founded a fort close to the area known as Corn Island, which was near the Falls of the Ohio. The Falls have always posed a problem for travelers of the Ohio River. Seemingly impassable for the most part, travelers were forced to get off on one side, travel around, and then board again on the other side of the Falls. Corn Island would lie at the head of the Falls if it still existed today. Instead it lays underneath the waters of the Ohio River today, just one more victim of man's greed. The island had been plundered for rock, which was used for cement. When a dam flooded in the 1920s, Corn Island was destroyed. Yet, it is remembered still as one of the earliest places that was settled by General

Clark and would lead him not long after to found a city that does remain today — Louisville.

While Kentucky plays a small, but important part in the birth of our nation, I find it interesting that so many Kentuckians are not even aware that Kentucky is not even a "state." Perhaps it was because of our close bond with Virginia that we chose to follow her example, setting ourselves apart from the first original thirteen colonies that did choose to be called states. Kentucky and Virginia are only two of four places that chose instead to be called a "Commonwealth." The etymology of the word *commonwealth* dates back to the fifteenth century and the word was *common weal.* The literal meaning of the word meant that the "common weal" was for the common good. In a larger frame of reference, if a place was dedicated to the "common well being" it was designated to be for the good of the common person and not just dedicated to the good of wealthy land owners or the overlords of an authoritarian state. We chose to be called the "Commonwealth of Kentucky" for exactly that reason. Commonwealth is all-inclusive and works for what is good for everyone, regardless of his or her background or socio-economic status.

Now you might be wondering what all this history and "Jeopardy!" styled trivia about the state has to do with its architecture and buildings. However, I stand by the fact that unless one knows how something begins, it's almost impossible to understand the artistic or cultural underpinnings that represent the growth and change of a society or community. Unless there is a small background where one can understand the importance of a river community to the trade and businesses of a district, it is highly unlikely that there will be any real insight or understanding of why and how a home can be constructed to suit both a business and personal need. In attempting to build a foundation of knowledge about the history of the state, I do hope that the details shed some light later on the methods and mindset of the architects and designers of the buildings in our city.

The etymology of the words "Kentucky" and "Louisville" are interesting side notes in the history of our area and are, I think, good stories to know, for they reflect the cultural duality of our community. There is a co-mingling of the European and Native American throughout the city, but nowhere is this more evidenced than in the names we find on the signs that remind us each time we turn down a lovely, tree lined street. Names such as Chicksaw Park, Cherokee Gardens, Seneca Park, and Iroquois Park all serve as constant, yet quiet voices that remind us softly, "Do not forget us. We were once here." The word "Kentake" has multiple variations of meaning depending on whom you ask; but most teachers of Social Studies or Kentucky Studies still hold onto General George Rogers Clark's translation of the word as being "river of blood." Some say that this refers to the Ohio River and its treacherous waters. However, another possible translation, and one that my father taught me as we rode along a dark stretch of Kentucky highway one night, was that "Kentake" meant "the dark and bloody ground." He explained to me that the Native Americans called it that because of all the blood that had been spilled when the white men came in and took their land. He said that there were massacres and that even Daniel Boone's son had been kidnapped and later killed because of the trespassing of white men onto Native American territory. While it's true that Boone's son was murdered in this way, it's just as true that the whole "dark and bloody ground" translation may be apocryphal. But, teachers still teach it much the way we tell children that George Washington chopped down the cherry tree. {*Note to reader: George Washington never chopped down the tree. It was a story invented by a Mr. Weams to extol the virtues of telling the truth in a way that children could understand and would, hopefully, want to emulate.*} Yet, just as we cling to the stories that we love, whether they are true or not, teachers still teach the translation and children continue to have their interest in history piqued, just as mine was way back in the old days. What scholars *do* agree on is that Kentake is indeed a Native American word and is likely Iroquois, Seneca, or Algonquin. There is a great probability that all of these groups would have been present in this area at some point in time. While they may not have had their actual nation here in its entirety, representatives could have been here and staked a claim to the territory in the name of the nation.

Although it is the largest city in Kentucky, Louisville is not the capital. The capital city is actually Frankfort, which was established in 1786. Contrary to popular belief, Frankfort was not named after the great city in Germany. According to legend, a group of settlers were making salt at the Kentucky River. All settlers new to the area knew in advance that they would have to contend with the Native groups and that they would likely attempt to drive the settlers from the land they believed was theirs. In the past, Native Americans struck out at white settlers, injuring or killing them, in hopes that this would deter others from invading their territories. In this case, Natives struck out at the settlers, killing a man by the name of Stephen Frank. The tract of land on which Frank died was known afterwards as "Frank's Ford" or Frankfort. Louisville, on the other hand, represents the epitome of European grandeur and elegance. Named for one of the most scandalous regimes in history, Louisville was named for King Louis XVI of France. At the time, the French had been very friendly with Americans, assisting them with money, supplies, and ammunition so that we could fight, and defeat, a common enemy — the British. However, poor Louis did not have the foresight nor the imagination to see how destructive his actions would turn out to be. He and his queen, Austrian born Marie Antionette, were only concerned with how to weaken and embarrass the English. By helping a rag-tag group of farmers and settlers strike out and gain their right to self-govern, Louis believed he was doing a great service to humanity. However, what he did not see was that he was a monarch just the way George the Third was king in England. As the people of France continued to starve, Louis would send money and supplies to the rebels, the people who had the nerve to stand up and tell their king that they were not going to allow him to govern them any longer. This started the French people thinking about whether or not *they* needed a king and they began to see Louis and Marie as enemies of the common good instead of Divinely born rulers sent from God. They watched their King give money to people who wanted to rule themselves — and then oppress the people of his own country by collecting taxes and punishing social dissidents by sending them to the Bastille. It was not long before the people revolted, beginning a bloody revolution that would end up costing Louis and Marie not only their crowns, but their heads, as well.

If you are, by chance, traveling anywhere in the world and you happen to mention that you are from Kentucky, you will invariably get one of two replies of recognition. One might be something along the lines of, "Oh, yes! The Kentucky Derby." The other reply appears to be the default understanding of our state and that would be, "Ahhhh! Kentucky Fried Chicken!" Yes, it is true. While we are the hometown of the "Greatest Two Minutes in Sports," nothing says "I come from Kentucky" like lard and deep fried fowl. But, we Kentuckians love both and are extremely proud of our Derby and all the celebrations that prelude the big race on the first Saturday in May. I would be remiss if I did not include a little blurb about the Derby, since it's the closest thing we have to a Mardi Gras here in Kentucky and it really does draw the majority of tourists to our town every year. While people may come to see the bourbon distilleries and visit the horse parks in Lexington, nothing says, "Come spend your money in our fair city" like a good old-fashioned horse race, replete with ladies in bountiful hats and gentlemen in silk ties. The home of the Derby would be the twin-spired towers of Churchill Downs and there is nothing more exciting than watching the trainers and jockeys lead the enormous thoroughbreds from their stalls to the point we call the "Winners Circle" to be photographed. The smell of the horses mixes with excitement and the possibility of winning a little money — and when all three come together with some mint julep soaked patrons, you have a winning combination for a day of racing that you will never forget.

As a small child I remember trying to understand if there was anything that was particularly *special* about where I lived. I must have been about five years old because I remember riding in the front seat of my father's big green pickup truck and standing up (these were the days before seatbelt laws) on the seat between my parents. I listened as they talked about the places around town where they spent their youth and the places that were no longer there. They reminisced about the memories they shared and I heard the regret in their voices when they mentioned places that had been torn down because they had fallen into extreme disrepair. There was a sense of pride that was instilled in my child's mind, a pride in where I lived and there was a feeling that our city was special and at one time, at least, had something to offer the rest of the world. Even then I was trying to find a way to understand the pride they felt and negotiate my own sense of belonging in our community. What was this that I was supposed to feel? What did it mean to have *Southern hospitality*? I had no idea at the time, but today I have a very deep and profound respect for those things that I could barely put a finger on back then. Community related pride is something that doesn't even have to be spoken; it's a silent nod among family members when they talk about the old places and their memories of them. It's a reverent smile when we sing "My Old Kentucky Home" right before the trumpeter plays the "Call to the Post" before the big Derby race. It's the butterflies that you feel when the horses are released and you know that yours is in front, two lengths ahead of all the others, and you know that the Derby jackpot is going to belong to you this year. Yet, even with all that, it is still something more. I asked my mother one year what Kentucky was famous for — other than the Derby. Without missing a beat she said, "Fast horses, smooth whiskey, and beautiful women." To this day, whenever I am asked where I am from, I always find a way to work my mother's cogent reply into my own.

The "River City," as Louisville is often called, reserves a special spot in the history of the United States, as it played an important role in the formative years of our country and was a participant in many of the conflicts that decided the fate of nations and people. Louisville's location on the river made it a prime spot for both slave traders and those escaping on the Underground Railroad. I always find it ironic that one waterway held both captivity and the promise of freedom—it just depended on which side you were banked. While many history classes teach that once runaway slaves reached the northern territories of Ohio and Indiana they were home free because those were considered "free states," nothing could be farther from the truth. Slave catchers were free to travel into the free states to bring back the "property" of the slave owners and it was nothing for a slave catcher to track a runaway slave up into Canada, even as far as Nova Scotia. If the slave did not find abolitionists or sympathizers along the way, they ran a great risk of being caught and returned to their former owners. Kentucky was a border state when it came to the issue of slavery. The closer one came to the river and the northernmost parts of the state, the more abolitionists and sympathizers one would find. In the more rural parts of the state, closer to the Tennessee border, one found more people who believed it in their best interest to side with those who wanted to keep Kentucky a slave state, since their resources and land were tied to the free labor. The river continued to be, however, an integral passage for those seeking freedom from oppression at the hands of others. As stated, the river was only a small part of achieving freedom. There needed to be what were called "Safe Houses" along the way. If a person could make it to a safe house, a home where they could rest, eat, and wait for a safe time to travel to the next house on the Underground Railroad, then the chances of actually making it to freedom increased. There is one known safe house that is listed in this book, the Brawner House, and there were stories of others. I had hoped to find evidence that the Squire Earick House was used for this purpose, as I had heard and read stories of a secret passage. However, when I checked with historians who are restoring the home, my source stated that this story couldn't be verified.

ARCHITECTURAL STYLES

In Louisville, neighborhoods were often categorized by ethnicity or occupation, as those who had things in common, whether it be language or occupation, would gather close together. People tend to gravitate toward what they understand and feel comfortable with. As the old saying goes, "Like must have like." Butchertown is self-explanatory, as is Germantown. Portland, as the name suggests, was a port side town for those who traveled up and down the Ohio River. The Highlands were not Scottish residents, but was established for those who sought higher ground and wanted to be out of the harmful path the river took when it flooded and destroyed everything in its wake. All these places were sprinkled with old families and new immigrants, all seeking to make a life and a home for those they loved. Interestingly, the homes, churches, businesses, and buildings reflect the socio-economic status of the owner and it would not be unusual for one street to have the same architectural style of home, for instance Italianate, but have the two homes constructed of different materials and one be much more ornate than the other. Even among equals, people found a way to set themselves apart based on affluence and success. The architecture discussed here will focus heavily on the following styles: Italianate, Gothic Revival, Beaux Arts, Richardsonian Romanesque, Queen Anne, Neo-Classical, Federalist, Georgian, and Chateauesque. I have not included the downtown district because of time and space. However, I am including a small explanation of the Modern/Post Modern architectural styles for reference only. Additionally, I added a short section I like to call my "Historic Etceteras." I tended to focus heavily on the districts that I love the most and that I feel have the most beautiful and interesting structures.

I believe that it is helpful for anyone who loves Louisville or the study of architecture to have a bit of a "cheat sheet" when looking at buildings around town. While specific details will be pointed out for each building discussed herein, it's important to know the particular aspects of each style so that one can take the information here and use it to identify structures outside the Louisville area and, in particular, in whatever area one chooses to call home.

This Historic Landmark building in Butchertown is an excellent example of Italianate structure.

Italianate — circa 1845 to approximately 1870

The American spirit has a special knack for taking European ideas and reinventing them in order to create our own unique interpretation. It appears to be our way of saying, "anything you can do, we can do better." The American variation on a theme, if you will, is no better evidenced than in the architecture of our cities. The Italianate structures, for example, were made popular in England, where it was originally known as "picturesque" architecture. The British designers were inspired by the villas and homes of the Italian Renaissance and reproduced something similar to that within the confines of a busy British city. However, American architects are clever and innovative individuals. They saw great opportunity in mass producing this architectural style and knew that it would be a style of building that could be a home or an office building. In mass production there is always the realization that much money can be made, as pieces are produced in large quantities and then assembled quickly. The opportunity for financial gain lay in the ability of the manufacturers to produce the ironwork that was needed for the internal structure very quickly and relatively cheaply. The rest of the homes could be constructed in the Italianate style with almost any material, so depending on the finances of the owner one could have a very elaborate structure or a relatively modest one. The main reason that this style became so popular was that it could fit almost any budget. It is interesting to me that the Italianate style was not popularized in the Deep South. Some historians speculate that this is because the Civil War intervened during the height of this style's popularity and consequently,

Italianate style buildings are not extremely common in that area. Even after the war was over and despite the cost-effectiveness of the materials one would need to build this type of structure, the South was still economically devastated, crippling its ability to rebuild, as most people would have liked. Since Louisville was close in proximity to the North and still remained a river city where trade and business boomed, it did not appear to experience the same level of economic hardships as the rest of the southern cities.

There are specific traits to look for when identifying Italianate structures. A few of these would be:

- · Low-pitched or flat roof
- · Balanced, symmetrical rectangular shape
- · Tall appearance with 2,3, or 4 stories
- · Wide overhanging eaves with brackets and **cornices**
- · Square **cupola**
- · Porch top with **balustrade** balconies
- · Tall, narrow double paned windows with hood moldings
- · Side bay windows
- · Heavily molded double doors
- · Roman or segmented arches above the windows and doors

Gothic Revival — circa 1830-1860

Gothic Revival is a personal favorite of mine because it reminds me so much of an Europe that exists for me only in history books and pictures. Since many people never get the chance to walk through the buttressed ceilings of Notre Dame du Paris or feel the warmth of the sunlight as it streams through the Rose Window, the Gothic Revival style of architecture allows us to experience this without having to leave our city. It is called Gothic Revival for almost this exact reason, as a matter of fact. It was a "re-birth" of the Gothic style of the middle ages and has also been referred to as "Neo-Gothic" in some circles. No matter what one chooses to call it, there is no denying that once again Americans have taken an European concept and style, reinvented it to suit our purposes, and then expanded upon it to gave it our own, personal spin. One will find this as a dominant style for churches and cathedrals in the early to mid 1800s, but it is not reserved for ecclesiastical purposes. The Inn at Woodhaven, which was constructed as a private residence, is an excellent example of Gothic Revival architecture adapted for a private dwelling. However, what is interesting about this style is that if one remembers that History 101 class from years ago, the Gothic Revival style will remind you that religion played an immense role in the lives of Medieval men and women. The churches of the Middle Ages *[side note: when we speak of "the church," this refers to the Catholic Church, as there was no other recognized Christian church in Europe until 1517 and Martin Luther's reformation. This term also excludes Jewish temples, synagogues, and Muslim mosques due to the fact that their architecture and construction were based on other principles of design and were designed in a specific way for other*

St. Joseph's Cathedral, Lousiville, Kentucky.

religious and symbolic reasons] took center stage in the lives of the common man. It was a place that was used to edify and educate the masses, which were mostly illiterate. How does one go about the business of educating those who cannot read or write? How does the church instruct them as to the rules of correct behavior and keep them in line with the teachings of the church if the people cannot read what is expected of them? The church structure itself was used as a tool for instructing the masses of people. The architecture of the church took on significant spiritual meaning, and the handiwork of man was meant to reflect the perfection of God and stand as a reflection of His goodness to the common person. The immense spires draw the eye upward toward heaven, where man's ultimate reward resides. Lofty ideals and contemplations should be elicited from people as they gaze upon things that are greater than themselves, hopefully bringing increased spiritual awareness and the desire to be better Christians. Stained glass, while beautiful to behold, also served a practical purpose for the people who came to worship. In order to teach the Bible stories and parables that would encourage them to lead good and holy lives, there had to be a visual representation. The people had to be able to see those who had come before them and from whom they were supposed to model their behavior, one day making it to Heaven to be with the saints and God. The multi-faceted panes of stained glass would let the sunlight into the churches, lighting up the room with scenes of spirituality and serenity. While beautiful to behold, it served a practical purpose for the people who came to worship. The priests were extolling the rewards of a virtuous life, but the people were unable to read the stories of those whom they were supposed to pattern their lives. It was primarily for the education of the common man that the windows were constructed, towering over the congregation in scenes larger than life. If the saints could endure the hardships of persecution and the horrors of martyrdom, how much more should the peasant be thankful for his or her present condition? Gothic architecture had another purpose in the lives of medieval man. Not only functioning as a means of visual education, the heavy stone structures also represented a sense of permanence in a world where nothing remained the same. People were born; people died. The church buildings remained. It would not be a stretch for American architects to take this concept and adapt it, which is what they did in Gothic Revival architecture. If one realizes that Gothic Revival had a specific purpose when it was employed as an architectural style, then it becomes easier to understand why we would have used it here in America. When Gothic Revival became popular in America, we were still craving legitimacy as a nation. We wanted to be taken seriously as a powerful nation in the same way that people had always viewed the old countries of Europe, like France, England, and Germany. The designers and architects would have been well aware that the heavy limestone and cut rock that held the buildings of the Middle Ages together, keeping them in tact throughout wars and natural disasters, lent a sense of legitimacy to the nations that housed them. In the same respect, people who designed American structures would have wanted buildings that reminded onlookers of the "Old World" and all its grandeur. If Europe's cathedrals and castles were what the rest of the world viewed as spectacular, then America could – and would – do the same. It's not a far stretch to imagine that the architects and designers of the early to mid-nineteenth century would have known or felt this cultural phenomenon and realized that what lent legitimacy to the other nations is what was old and established. Many of the churches in France were older than we were as a nation. Europe had ancient buildings, libraries, and cathedrals that made them seem venerable in the eyes of the world. The Old World countries represented wealth, power, and fortitude. They were successful. They had enough money to construct titanic buildings and these became the benchmarks of achievement. Therefore, inventive as we are, we took one aspect of European culture and history and gave it our own Yankee Doodle spin. We wanted the rest of the world to know we were not a flash in the pan democracy. We were here to stay and become a force to be reckoned with. We were on the world power scene *permanently.* We took the Gothic Revival and made it our own. Author Carrie Ann Powell notes that permanency was a very important aspect of Gothic Revival style when she states:

> The structures built in the Gothic architectural style had such of a powerful effect because of the symbolism behind them. The Gothic architecture design was used to symbolize permanence and authority for public buildings. Because of the writings of Pugin and Ruskin, Gothic architecture was increasingly associated with both Christianity and truthfulness (Girouard, 273). The cathedral was supposed to be the **image of the Christian Universe**. The cathedral was the "House of God, the dwelling place of his mystical person" (Grodecki, 14). The multicolored stained-glass

windows have been compared to the precious stones encrusted in the walls of the New Jerusalem. In the nineteenth century, the full-blooded Gothic Architecture Revival sought to revitalize Christian society by a return to the cultural values of the Middle Ages (Jenner, 24). In the 1830s, church reformers in England sought to revive the Anglican liturgy by modeling new buildings in the style of the medieval parish churches. "These simple solemn buildings were intended to fuse function and symbolism by representing in wood and stone a holierness, less secular kind of religious life, the theology and tradition of ancient church cleansed of eighteenth century rationalism" (Lane, 208). Every medieval church was supposed to be an evocation of the heavenly Jerusalem, the abode of the saved, to be established after the completion of the Last Judgment (Wilson, 8). In England, the Gothic house stood for good principle and good cheer. (Powell, 1995)[1]

Specific characteristics of Gothic Revival are:
- Asymmetrical in style
- Steeply gabled roof
- Stained glass
- Buttresses on the inside
- **Foils** (including trefoil, quatrefoil, etc.)
- **Battlements**
- **Finials** atop the spires
- **Gothic**, arched windows and some gingerbread
- Pinnacles, tracery, ribs
- Vaults, pendants, and oriel windows

Neo-Classical — circa 1750-1880

The Neo-Classical Era in architecture was a reinterpretation of classical ancient Greek and Roman styles. After the flowery and ornate styling of the Baroque and Rococo styles, there was a longing to return to cleaner, simpler lines and forms. The triangular pediments, the long columns, and often the domed roof would remind onlookers that there was a renewed interest in the classical world. Revived interest in classical works, archaeology of the ancient world, and the symbolic rebirth of Rome in the form of the United States gave architects and brilliant designers fodder for creating many of our nation's most beloved buildings. A return to logic and that which made sense, like men governing themselves instead of being governed by a king, was prevalent in this new nation, and men like Thomas Jefferson and Pierre L'Enfant wanted to make sure that this country's buildings and architecture reflected the balance and symmetry of a neatly ordered governmental system. Modeled after the Republic of Rome, many of the United States' most important residences, libraries, schools, and political structures are constructed in the Neo-Classical style. As a side note, both Federalist and Greek Revival were strongly influenced by the Neo-Classical style. Since Neo-Classical is a much simpler form of architecture when compared to something like Gothic Revival, the list of "look fors" is much shorter.

Specific traits of the Neo-Classical structure could be:
- · Symmetrical construction
- · Tall columns
- · Pediments
- · Domes

Richardsonian Romanesque — circa 1870-1900

If Americans have one style that is unique to us, it might just be Richardsonian Romanesque. Named for its creator, architect Henry Hobson Richardson, this style is a mixture of Spanish and French intertwined with Italian Romanesque. It is a style that is heavy and simply takes your breath away when you stand before it. The material is often heavy, rough stone and reminds one of a great castle or European cathedral. Richardson had studied in Europe, so the influence of the architecture there and its durability and stability had a profound impact on his own work. The Richardsonian Romanesque style is so durable and the materials are usually so heavy that one stands in awe and wonders if there is anything short of a massive earthquake that could bring such a structure to the ground. The turrets – and there is usually at

Holland Tax House.

Close-up of turret on the Holland Tax House.

least one – are often made of heavy stone or brick and are open, leading to a balustrade. These fantastically constructed, castle-looking structures pique one's imagination, teleporting our senses and thoughts through time to these balconies where elegantly dressed young ladies gracefully entertained dapper young gentlemen coming to court them in the cool of the evening.

The Richardsonian Romanesque can be characterized by the following features:

- · Massive stone walls
- · Dramatic semicircular arches.
- · Heaviness is ever-present throughout the structure
- · Stone construction
- · Deep windows
- · Cavernous recessed door openings
- · Bands of windows
- · Contrasting color and texture of stone
- · Unusual sculptured shapes in stone
- · Short, robust columns
- · Towers occur in about 75 percent of Richardson's buildings. A second tower occurs in roughly 15%.[2]

Private residence on St. James Court.

Queen Anne — circa 1880-1910

While Queen Anne typically denotes a very feminine aspect to design it should be noted that this showy, ornately decorated style actually gained momentum at the height of the Industrial Revolution in America. Once the machines that could make interchangeable parts began to create pre-fabricated moldings and pieces for these beautiful gingerbread houses, it was much easier for the common person to acquire a home that was styled after those occupied by the leaders of the industry. So while America worked away, becoming an industrial giant, factory owners and industry leaders wanted to make certain that everyone was aware of the prosperity and the benefits reaped from "Good Ole Yankee Know-How." Therefore, their homes were ornate, with scalloped shingles on the sides, towers with soft, feminine curves to them, turned spindle work on the front porches, and rounded arches at the windows. Some critics label this a "feminine" architectural style, presumably due to the connotations associated with bearing a female's name. Yet, that is not the only reason, I am sure. The softly rounded, delicate features that make the style appealing to the eye parallel the physical characteristics that the Victorians so cherished. Demure, yet eye-catching curves, slender fixtures that taper at the bottom, intricate, and lovely adornments that grace the figure of the home were all descriptions that could easily be attributed to the ladies of the time, making this style fetching, leaving the on-looker wanting more. This Victorian "eye candy" is typically what we think of when we envision Victorian architecture and it was used mostly in residences. In sharp contrast to the roughness of Richardsonian Romanesque or the piercing spires and sharp, pointed arches of the Gothic Revival, Queen Anne style evokes feelings of warmth and accessibility. There are no castle-like fortresses that must be battered down. Queen Anne homes silently beckon you to the front porch to sit, quietly admiring their beauty, and have a glass of lemonade. The materials used reflect warmth that is often felt as "feminine." It is nearly impossible to include every small detail associated with the Queen Anne style due to the many variations on the style. Small details can be altered to please individual preferences. Additionally, as with most styles, there are characteristics that are shared. It must be noted that this list is not all-inclusive, since there are so many variations of this style it would be a long list indeed if we attempted to include everything.

Queen Anne overlaps with characteristics from a few other architectural styles, but some of the more dominant features are:

- Elaborate gingerbread trim
- "Fish scale" shingle patterns
- Circular tower or turret with a "candle-snuffer" roof
- Machine turned spindles on porches
- Steeply pitched roof
- Often bay or rounded arch windows[3]

Modern and Post-Modern — circa 1900-present

Modern and Post-Modern architecture are the most difficult to characterize and some of the easiest to identify, as there is no set pattern that the architect or designer must follow. Springing up from the aftermath – and the success – of the Industrial Revolution, Modern architecture again reveals the necessity for reinvention of the old. Modern architecture behaves like youth from every generation. It attempts to re-define itself in a very deconstructionist manner. People will know what it is by looking at what it is not. If a building has a turret, but no fish scale shingling, then it is not really Queen Anne. If the building is made of heavy stone, but does not have the other features of Richardonian Romanesque, then what on earth could it possibly be? And, moreover, why would someone build a structure that looks like that? It is almost as if I can hear the other older, "grandmotherly" homes speaking to each other, whispering about the strange newcomer to the block, gossiping about what it must have under its floorboards:

> *"You know that new building, the one on Elm? I heard that she has no trim and she's made of steel. I can't imagine anyone finding that attractive. Nothing soft about her. Can you imagine? She probably won't even have windows with stained glass."*
>
> *"Yes, I heard the same thing. She probably wants everyone in town to be able to see in. You know how those kinds of places are. Fast. Can you imagine? What is the neighborhood coming to when we let her kind in?"*

Younger generations define themselves by what they wear and wear accoutrements that set them apart from the previous generation. Modern architects and the offspring of their imaginations do exactly that — namely, reject the constructs and designs of the previous generation in order to establish a new, rejuvenated identity separate from that of their predecessors. The upstart Modernist movement established the importance of the form of the structure following the function it would serve. Often, the building would boast minimalist aspects and its simplicity of form identifies it as a Modern structure. This style is often seen in looming skyscrapers, bastions of concrete and steel, that silently speak the metaphor of the strength, power, and unconquerable nature of a prosperous, industrialized nation. Post-Modern architecture was a response to the stark functionality of modernism. Tired of buildings that had no personality, architects wanted to demonstrate their intellectual and artistic prowess by creating buildings that appealed not only to those who valued function, but creativity as well. Post-Modernists believed that the structures they built should have a pleasing aesthetic, as well as a logical form and function. They had tired of the boring concrete and steel facades of the previous movement in architecture and longed for an integration of what they saw as necessary with what they felt was interesting. With the Post-Modern architecture, you will often see the personality of the architect shine through the building, almost as if it were a fingerprint left behind.

This view is a nice example of Post-Modern architecture in the Downtown District.

Modern architecture can be identified by the following:

- A rejection of historical styles as a source of architectural form (historicism)
- An adoption of the principle that the materials and functional requirements determine the result
- An adoption of the machine aesthetic
- A rejection of ornament
- A simplification of form and elimination of "unnecessary detail"
- An adoption of expressed structure
- Form follows function[4]

Some characteristics of Post-Modern architecture, as described by Michael Leland include:

Contextualism: Where Modern buildings tended to only focus on a building's site, postmodern architecture complemented a building's surroundings through its design. This could include the building's placement on its site as well as the materials used in the building.

Allusionism: Postmodern architecture looks to past architecture styles for inspiration. It attempts to use modern technology and historical design to create buildings that will be more accessible to the general public.

Ornamentalism: Where Modernism rejected applied ornamentation, Postmodernism uses ornament and color to create a building that will draw attention and be identifiable by those who view it.[5]

Reviewing and identifying specific characteristics of architectural styles represented here is necessary when attempting to understand the time period in which a building was constructed. The importance of style, design, values, and beliefs all come together in a neat package forged by bricks, stone, or wood. Within the framework of the building lie many keys that unlock the secrets of a culture. It is through examination and appreciation of the exterior that we connect with what – or whom – resides/ resided in the interior. When it comes right down to the nitty gritty, the names, faces, and stories of the people – ***real people*** – who lived, loved, and often died in these buildings are the real heart of this book. While it is interesting to see a familiar place and be able to say, "Ah, yes…that is a typical representation of a Queen Anne style home, popularized in the 1880s. You can tell because of the so-called 'candle snuffer' atop the tower," it really does not speak to what is truly interesting—the stories behind the areas and the people who lived there.

Chapter One:

DOWNTOWN LOUISVILLE

The business district of downtown Louisville goes in so many different directions that it would be impossible to give equal time to each and every architectural goodie that I pass on a daily basis. Main Street, however, gives a nice picture of what things were like at the turn-of-the-century. The Italianate structures were symmetrical and many local businesses called Main Street their home. Many still do. The city still appears to be a good blend of the old and the new. The old buildings are being refurbished as urban lofts and many younger people are choosing to make the downtown district their home. Conveniently located near shopping districts, local hospitals, several universities, including the University of Louisville, the downtown district appeals to the movers and shakers of the business arena. If you look at the Louisville skyline, however, it would not be the old buildings that would catch your eye first, but rather the tall post-modern skyscrapers. The Aegon building pierces the sky with its large, domed top. Glowing a soft yellow in the early morning light, its position on the cityscape is without a doubt the focal point. The Humana Building appears on the scene like a post-modern interpretation of a Mesopotamian ziggurat. The sleek walls and zigzags at the top make the Humana building a site to behold whether you are on the ground looking at the rose and pink granite or on the balcony overlooking the Ohio River.

CAST IRON

Although I could not believe it when I first uncovered the information, but much of Main Street and the business facades are not stonework or masonry as I had assumed they were. The facades are actually made of cast iron, making Louisville the second largest cast-iron city in America. Soho in New York is number one. I could not believe that I just took it for granted that the buildings were plaster, brick, and stone. There really is no way to tell, unless you are looking for it, but I found that in the second half of the nineteenth century, cast iron became a very popular material for building facades as it could easily be painted and it lasted a long, long time. Districts such as the cast-iron district in Louisville are really unidentifiable, as there is often no outward appearance of the metal itself. It was, like our nation, strong and durable. Since steel had not come onto the scene yet, cast iron was believed to be one of the strongest materials with which to construct large buildings, bridges, and factories. However, what the builders and architects did not know at the time was the one major flaw of all cast iron structures. If a fire were to break out, as it did in many large factories both here and in England, the cast iron would weaken

and bend or break. It was not, as some people mistakenly named it, "fireproof." Fire was, it would appear, the Achilles heel of this modern construction wonder material. Many buildings collapsed on themselves and the girders that were used in construction melted, bent, or broke during exposure to extreme heat. Yet, on a positive note, the cast iron did allow for good support if no heat was present, and consequently more windows could be installed, letting in more natural light. From an artistic perspective, cast iron could also be used in frontal facades because of its bendable properties. Twisting cast iron into beautiful designs for the front of a building was a popular device, as they could be painted a multitude of colors and the material was extremely long lasting — in the absence of fire or extreme heat, of course.

FRAZIER INTERNATIONAL HISTORY MUSEUM

The Louisville Slugger Museum and the Frazier Historical Arms Museum also add to the cultural heritage of the city.

The Brown family name is one of the most familiar to those of us who have lived here for awhile. The Brown Hotel, among other sites, serves as a reminder of the family whose philanthropy and concern for their city has given us some of the most precious and rare collections of historical artifacts in our museums today. Additionally, the Browns are renowned as a family of givers. They have given to the community and universities, contributed to the hospitals and research centers, including but not limited to Jewish Hospital and the Frazier Rehab Center, and acted as true ambassadors of our city. Tied locally to the Brown-Foreman company, Owsley Brown Frazier took what was formerly an abandoned warehouse and converted it into one of the

Frazier International History Museum is located on "Museum Row." It is the last building before the overpass and is recognized by the beautiful dome-shaped turret.

quiet treasures of our city. The 75,000-square foot space houses both a small movie theatre and an auditorium, which serves the needs of local educators and visitors alike with such exhibits as the recent display, "A Slave Ship Speaks." Visitors were able to view and in some way try to understand the experiences of slaves that took the trip on the ship called the *Henrietta Marie*. Many artifacts that were gathered from the ship are instrumental in piecing together the horrifying journey that the people took and the museum has been instrumental in bringing historical awareness to the community.

The museum is unlike any other in Louisville, housing many primary sources of information and artifacts, such as guns previously owned by George Washington, Teddy Roosevelt, and the outlaw, Jesse James. The museum offers an incredible journey of discovery into the past, and in doing so, allows its visitors to understand the present.

The building itself is located on what is locally known as "Museum Row." Part of the "cast iron" district, the façade has been redone and can be recognized by the dome-shaped turret. But, for the turret, which is not particularly recognizable as an Italianate characteristic, the rest of the building fits the Italianate description. The flat roof, rounded windows, and over hung molding are all designs that are typical of the style.

Chapter Two:
BUTCHERTOWN

If you read only historical excerpts of how the district known as "Butchertown" received it's oh-so-apropos moniker, then you would be missing out on some of the really neat historical anecdotes that have lain buried away in the memories of those who actually lived there in its heyday. In the days before air conditioning, when people had to sit outside in the summer to cool off, friends, neighbors, and family members were never more than a fence row or a short walk along the tree-lined streets away. This is the Butchertown my mother remembers. Her mother, her grandmother, aunts, uncles, cousins, were like many of the people in Butchertown, German immigrants who lived in an area where those around them spoke their language and where they felt at ease and at home. She told so many times of walking from one grandmother's house to the other, stopping for hot doughnuts fresh from the corner bakery. "You could smell those doughnuts from blocks away," she said, "and in the war years we were always hungry. But, somehow one of my grandmothers always found enough money to get two or three."

Butchertown, however, was not a place remembered as being the sweetest smelling district in the city. The Bourbon Stockyards Slaughterhouse was just a few blocks away and, as the city's name suggests, the local butchers found it easy and relatively costless to discard unused animal remains into Beargrass Creek. The creek had been rerouted away from the downtown Louisville business district for exactly that reason. The stench from the rotting remains would have made it a highly unpleasant place to either work or shop, so it was necessary to divert it elsewhere. Many German families, like that of my great grandmother, Minnie Schneider, came to Butchertown to find those who were like them, and also to find work. It was a thriving community until the 1937 flood destroyed most of the businesses and ran many of the residents out of their homes to higher ground. There are many former residents who remember a dead cow getting caught in the top most branches of a tree, finding it only after the flood water subsided, and a house floating down the middle of Adams Street. The water was so high that many people were unable to rebuild, which some people viewed as a blessing since the neighborhood had attracted a reputation for housing people who loved their liquor and a good fight…usually in that order. However, many of the homes withstood the flood damage and families were able to continue to live and thrive there.

A blot on the face of this neighborhood was an incident known as the "Bloody Monday" riots that occurred August 6, 1855. The Whig Party originally began in England, formed as an oppositional voice to autocratic rule. The original Whigs fought against the British in the American Revolution, aligning themselves with a "rule by the people" belief. After the Revolution, and in direct opposition to Andrew Jackson, the Whig Party gained strength as one half of the two-party system that Americans desired. Springing from old Federalist concepts, the Whig Party hailed the authority of Congress over that of the President. "King Andrew" (Andrew Jackson), as he was called by Whigs and critics alike, was unpopular due to the amount of executive power he wielded. Believing in strong states' rights, the group that was established as a voice against tyrannical rule in 1834 did not last, but did give our nation war heroes and Presidents, and reinforced the belief that keeping the powers of the Executive Branch in check was essential to democracy. Understanding that the Whig Party boasted many supporters from the Germantown area gives us a greater understanding of how the "Know Nothings" came to be so popular. Many former Whigs turned their attention to the problems in areas where they lived, which they blamed on immigration. In the 1830s to the 1860s, there was a large influx of German Catholics to the country and specifically, the area in Louisville, which would take the name "Germantown" for obvious reasons. Many of the residents viewed these newcomers as invaders, not true "Americans" since they were not born here. Looked upon with suspicion and derision as drunks and papists, the Protestant population fueled its bigotry and distrust with anti-immigration sentiments. Some groups of people were convinced that the Pope, at that time Pius IX, was behind the influx of Catholic immigrants and that he wanted to infuse Americans with Rome's agenda. Suspicions grew and secret organizations were formed. These organizations would meet secretly and when officials or outsiders would ask about these societies and the goings-on therein, their members would simply reply, "I know nothing." The "Know Nothing" party was formed and in the small neighborhood of Butchertown, mistrust and anger would lead to death and destruction. The so-called "Know Nothing" party killed twenty-two Irish and German Catholic immigrants in order to keep them and their ilk from voting in an election. As they went to the polls, they were threatened, beaten, and worse. Obviously, this was another way to mask the dominant prejudice and cultural intolerance against immigrants by saying that these people had no right to vote since they were not born here and many did not even speak the language. However, there were those who wanted nothing more than to have everyone view these people as second-class citizens. This was, of course, all done in the name of "true Americanism" and the small neighborhood filled with people who had come to America looking for a safe place and a new start, saw its streets filled with smoke from burning buildings, men shot in the head, and bodies hanging from makeshift gallows. Surviving the horrors of the Bloody Monday riots was a testament to true American spirit. Those who stayed refused to be intimidated and refused to run from their homes. Standing firmly on the belief that America was still the best place to build a life, they persevered and rebuilt as a community of survivors who would instill these values into future generations. The immigrant residents of Butchertown were likely no strangers to upheaval and violence. Coming from Ireland, where many Protestants and Catholics, yet today, still share a mutual distrust and aversion to one another, or Germany, where Protestantism was born with Martin Luther's original break with the Catholic Church in 1517, inhabitants of Butchertown might have viewed this as another growing pain that would one day lead to a life free from religious persecution and prejudice. Whatever they believed, one thing was certain — many had come too far and sacrificed too much in order to make a fresh start to allow others to run them out of their homes. The only choice was to stay and stick it out to the end.

Today, the ugliness of the past is far behind, except in the memories of local historians and those interested in a good story or two, and in its place came people who loved the area for the ties that they felt to it either by family or just plain love of the lovely homes that sit behind tree-lined streets. Community loyalty in Butchertown, as well as the ties to the homes and local businesses, allows residents and former residents to feel that they have a common interest in local activities. Recent preservation initiatives undertaken by city council members have gained much support with the home and business owners and many of the homes were added to the National Historic Registry due to their diligence. And, the family ties still remain as strong as ever, with homes being passed down from generation to generation. It's not uncommon for me to say to my mother that I happened upon a house today that used to be on Adam's Street (or any other street in the area) and have her reply with a wistful and excited voice, "Oh, yes! I know that house and the people who live there — if they live there still."

As much as I would like to fool myself into thinking I'm making huge discoveries about the area and the families who lived in or still occupy the homes there, I know I'm not. In the beginning, I naively believed I was forging fearlessly into previously untrodden territory wherein lies a wealth of undiscovered information, but I have to be honest with myself and you, my readers, by admitting that my mother is still the best source of information about her former stomping grounds. She can usually tell me much more than the local residents, websites, or famed historians of the area. Therein lies the treasure. It is in listening to the collections of memories and recollections of the older inhabitants and family story-keepers that we preserve our heritage, thereby enabling us to pass on these jewels of knowledge to our children, and in doing so, becoming the historians, ourselves.

Families who have ties to the local parish, St. Joseph's Catholic Church, or the former community center, Wesley House, keep coming back to work, worship, or visit. Even though the buttery goodness of Bakery Square, formerly Hellemueller's Bakery, ceased to waft down the alleyways to draw little girls and their grandmothers to their doors, people still find reasons to come and connect with a living, thriving part of Louisville's rich history.

HIEGOLD HOUSE

Of the many historic homes that still exist, one of the most famous is the Heigold House.

Technically, it is not even a "house" anymore, as the house part disintegrated over the years. Now, all that remains of this once grand structure is a façade, which sits in the parking lot of a local liquor store, awaiting its new home as the entryway to the Butchertown area. While architecturally and historically interesting, it is also a small anecdote in my personal family history. Family members, like most in the day, were laborers. My uncle, Jerry Offutt, came from a family of masons and it was his ancestors – a great, great grandfather – who made and laid the bricks of the Hiegold House. In its heyday, the Hiegold House, commissioned by stonemason Charles Heigold, was a sight to behold. A German immigrant, Charles wanted to build a monument to the greatness of this nation and its leaders. So taken was Mr. Hiegold with the government of the United States, and the greatness of the people who forged its liberty, that he longed to preserve his admiration for them in stone. He carved the heads of George Washington, the first President, and James Buchanan, the fifteenth President. Former President Millard Fillmore, who was the last Whig party president and therefore had ties to the Know Nothing party, helped in Buchanan's election to the presidency, defeating Republican John Freemont for the position. In knowing a little history of the Whigs and Know Nothings,

Hiegold House was a great building in its time. Unfortunately, all that is left to represent the pride that one man felt about his country and his opportunity to live the American dream, is the façade.

Detail of over-hung door molding with Washington's head carved above it. Additionally, we can see Buchanan's head larger and above that of Washington. Notice the symbolism of the women, likely representative of Justice and Liberty.

one can almost guess the politics of the designer, but I do wonder why Hiegold would have constructed a monument to someone who might have had ties to anti-immigration politics? Perhaps, an immigrant himself, he was simply glad to be in America and whatever President was in office was hailed as great because he was American. One can only guess at the reasons that Buchanan was included in so great a monument, when he was a President who really had no intention of ever being in that position and only reluctantly accepted his party's nomination. Never-the-less, Heigold preserved these faces from our nation's past, when one of them could have easily been overlooked except in the history books. The house itself was overlooked as a valuable historical marker. Over the years, it fell into disrepair and began to crumble until all that was left was the façade. Today, it has been declared an historic landmark and will be moved from its current location to Butchertown to act as a monument to the immigrants who came and made this neighborhood a wonderful part of the city. Very little is left of the actual building so it is difficult to discern what type of architectural style it would have taken. Since we know that the building's construction was finished in 1853, a good guess would probably be that this home was likely done in the Italianate style. With its over-hung, molded windows and symmetrical rectangular shape that rises two stories, it could fit the description. However, there is something inside of me that believes that there must have been some sort of Neo-Classical aspect to the building at some point in time. While this is just conjecture on my part, it would seem strange if there were no tribute to Thomas Jefferson and the ideals of the classical world represented somewhere in this home. While the building itself is silent on this matter, one can still speculate about other influences based on the information we know about the man. Charles Hiegold's sense of nationalism during an age of anti-immigration sentiments remains as much of a tribute to the American spirit as does the façade of his once stately home. It is likely that this is one reason people have been reluctant to do away with the remaining structure completely. As I have previously stated, architecture is such a valuable way to preserve the culture and beliefs of an era. The Heigold House is an excellent example of this. It stands as an important reminder of how those who immigrated to this country felt about having a new start and a chance at a great life. For example, in the detail of the house, James Buchanan's head looms largely over that of George Washington. Perhaps this was done to commemorate Buchanan while still paying tribute to the first President. Interestingly, other details really bring out the sense of American pride and nationalism that Heigold wanted represented for all to see. In the carving of Washington above the door molding, there are two women represented, one on either side. One carries the scales of justice and one holds a shield and spear. Likely, Heigold wanted to personify "liberty" and "justice" as two principle characteristics upon which our founding fathers, George Washington being one of them, would have relied heavily when creating the government. The eagle is also represented, as are thirteen stars, presumably one for each of the original thirteen colonies.

THOMAS EDISON HOUSE

When I first went looking for this house, I passed by it two or three times before I actually realized that the unassuming, little double shot-gun style home was right in front of my face. In all the years that I lived in Louisville, I never knew that Thomas Edison, inventor of the light bulb (among other things), had lived in my city from 1866-1867. He was very accomplished at sending and receiving telegraph messages and had absolutely no trouble landing a job at the Western Union telegraph office in Louisville. Edison had a fascination with the telegraph and spent much of this time trying to improve on it. Over the course of Edison's lifetime, he was issued 125 patents, including the patent for the first incandescent light bulb, the forerunner of what we use today when we flip on a light switch. The affects of this invention were far reaching in Louisville, going even further than the convenience of lighting that would make gas lighting relatively obsolete. It played a large part in the development and popularity of another Louisville area, Belgravia Court, after his invention was showcased at the Southern Exposition of 1883, which was held in Louisville. Edison's time in Louisville, however, was brief, mostly due to his own clumsiness. The spirit of invention that drove his desire to create was uncontainable and one evening, while working at the telegraph office, he experimented with some battery acid. Perhaps it was down time for him, or perhaps he was doing one thing when he should have been doing another, but whatever the reason, he was definitely experimenting on company time. While working with the acid, he spilled it on the floor, where it immediately began to eat through the floor. To make matters worse, of all offices to be under the floor, it had to be that of his boss. Edison was not a lucky man in this situation, as his boss's desk was directly under the hole in the floor, now eaten away by the acid, now dripping onto the desk. I did not find evidence to suggest that the acid kept eating away at the desk and the floor it sat on until it reached the other side of the earth, but the damage must have been considerable. He was dismissed from his position the next day and left Louisville shortly thereafter. While unrelated, I couldn't help wondering: "If a person could invent an acid that could eat through anything, what would they keep it in?"

The rooms that served as Edison's home during his short stay in Louisville are housed in a structure that, while historically valuable, is architecturally unassuming. The house serves as a small museum and one can see how it would have looked while Edison stayed there. It has historic items and Edison memorabilia. A film on Edison can be viewed while sitting in the very rooms he once called his own. The historians and curators are welcoming to visitors, speaking of the home and the contributions Edison made to both our community and the world at large. The home itself is red brick and could easily be missed. One could, as I did, pass right by it if it were not for the historic marker out in front. The double shotgun style was originally constructed as a duplex. Called a "shot-gun" style home, the name had nothing to do with violence in the area or the designer's propensity toward shooting guns. It is called this because it was constructed in a way that if one fired a shotgun through the front door, it would go right through the house and out the back door without ever hitting a wall. Shotgun homes are noted to be small, with the living area and the bedroom back-to-back, only separated by a doorway. But, as this was what Edison would have been able to afford on his salary, it is interesting to see the modest beginnings of one of America's greatest inventors.

The Thomas Edison House is located in Butchertown, the heart of the meat packing industry. The interior remains relatively unchanged. Visitors can see many of Edison's personal items and view a film about him while sitting in a room located right behind his bedroom.

WESLEY HOUSE

The Wesley House is one of the most beautiful Italianate structures in the entire Butchertown area. Constructed in the late nineteenth century, some of my research turned up information that in 1903, Mrs. Gross Alexander took the structure, which was formerly known as the Louisville Settlement House, and founded The Louisville Wesley House. According to the recorded history of the building, it was established by the mission's branch of the Methodist church as a caring outreach program to help the underprivileged. Their "mission statement" from 1903 reads:

> "It is a Christian home organized to provide a center for religious and philanthropic work, in the interest especially of a considerable class in the east end of our city's population that is more or less unreached by churches in their regular work...the work is evangelical and seeks not only to instruct but regenerate."
>
> **Neighborhood**: A mixed factory and tenement neighborhood. The people are of German and American descent, with a few Swiss and Jews. The tone of the district is Protestant-Evangelical, with there being only a limited number of Catholics. There is much overcrowding, poverty, intemperance, and employment of children.[6]

Some of this information I can verify as true, as my great-grandmother was a frequent user of the Wesley House's services. In addition to providing

Notice the ornate filigree ironwork that is original to the home. The intricate molding and bracing under the roof is also original and still in incredible condition despite having weathered the years and the elements.

This is leaded stained glass and is original to the home. The contractor noted that it is an interesting pattern because what you see depends on how you look at it! One might be able to see a mask or an old man's face in the glass.

milk, legal aid, and rummage sales, the Wesley House offered child care services even at the turn-of-the-century. This was extremely progressive since most women stayed home with their children and did not work. However, my great-grandmother, Minnie Schneider, had been left with two small children after her husband, James Prather, abandoned her. She was fortunate to be able to leave her two young daughters in the care of the people at the Wesley House so she could work and support her family. Sadly, when a man abandoned his wife and children in the early 1900s, there was little recourse for a woman who had few living relatives, especially since they lived in other areas of Louisville. Furthermore, Minnie was nine months pregnant with their third child when James left her for another woman. Tragically, this occurred during the influenza epidemic of 1916-1917. Shortly after he left, she delivered their third daughter, Margie, who died shortly after birth. Alone, devastated by the death of her infant, and with two other children she'd be raising alone, Minnie turned to the Wesley House for help. If it had not been for the childcare that they provided so that she could work, Minnie might have been another welfare case. Instead, the programs offered by the Wesley House allowed her to work and make a living for her family. I like to think that this kind of tenacity – the ability to overcome personal tragedy and eventually have success – is the legacy she left me. While I am certain that there is no shortage of personal success stories that the Wesley House contributed to, the ones that mean the most are always the ones that affect us personally. Times were difficult in those days. It was the age of the Depression and the Soup Line. People were starving in the streets and every day items, such as rubber bands or paper bags, were precious commodities. School was important and both of Minnie's girls, Catherine and Henrietta, my grandmother, attended St. Joseph's School until eighth grade. At that time, my grandmother quit school to go to work and help support the family. It was a common story, as many children did the same thing. Everyone had to work for the good – and the survival – of the family. The local Laundromat paid seven cents an hour and my grandmother worked there tirelessly, helping her mother, for ten or more hours every day. This information verified that child labor in the Butchertown area was a problem, but one must realize that these were the days before childhood was cherished and treasured as an innate right. Children from families all over were doing the exact same thing and child labor was an accepted practice. The Wesley House was a wonderful distraction for children in those days. They had social gatherings, Christmas functions, and were generally a respite for the children who worked tirelessly along with their parents. My grandmother always spoke well of those who ran the Wesley House. It is interesting that in this pre-dominantly Catholic neighborhood, there was a real sense of ecumenical concern that stemmed from the Wesley House. Concern for the well being of the entire neighborhood, no matter the faith of the person in need, was the primary objective. While the quote from the mission statement of Wesley House states that the demographic was primarily Protestant Evangelical, I do believe this is just wishful thinking on their part. With the strong following of St. Joseph Catholic Church, I wonder about the accuracy of the statement. What cannot be denied is that need knows no religious doctrine and whatever agenda the Wesley House may have originally had, it never showed in its actions. They served anyone in need and ministered to a community that greatly appreciated all they did for local families.

We know that the house dates at least back to 1871 because inside one of the fireplaces is an original plaque denoting when the fireplace was manufactured. Presuming that it was put into the home as a brand new appliance, this would give us a general date. That means these homes were likely built twenty to thirty years before the Wesley House took ownership of them.

Wesley House. Close up of original molding over the "daughter's house."

In my research, I never turned up any information about the former owners of the home. However, I was very blessed the day I shot the pictures of the Wesley House, because the contractor, who took a keen interest in the preservation of the beautiful structure, was very informed about the history of the building. It would appear that when it was first constructed, there was only one building. It was large and beautiful, with the most modern of conveniences, such as gas lighting. I was even able to see the original outlets for the gaslights. The staircase that leads up to the second and third floors is breathtakingly beautiful—even a hundred and fifty years later. It was most definitely built as a single-family dwelling. The servant's quarters were on the third floor, which would have been the warmest place in the house in the wintertime. The family lived there until one of the daughters married. Upon her marriage, the father built her a home right next door, with a walkway between the two houses so that the servants could travel between the two. This walkway, which is decorated with the original iron work that is typical of an Italianate home, was also known as a "whistling walkway" since the servants would be required to whistle as they carried food between the homes. This ensured that no food was pilfered by the servants along the way. I mused about the home that was built so close to the family abode. Why would the father insist on the daughter and her husband living so close? Was the husband "intemperate," and that worried the father? Was there a family illness that needed tending? It may be something as simple as what my mother said, "In those days, families stayed close. People didn't move away from each other. There was a closeness there that we don't have today." Perhaps this is true. But, I would like to think there is a much more dramatic or romantic story that lies buried in this home. What I noticed when I examined both houses was that the daughter's house was not as nice as the original one. The staircase was an exact replica of the original — but the quality was not as good. The living quarters were not as ornate, either. One can only wonder if the parents were making a statement by making the other house "not quite as good" as the home of origin. In my mind, I wondered if they were making a statement about the daughter's choice of husband. I wondered if it was for the safety of the daughter and any children that the parents built a home so close to the original. When you look out certain windows, you have a bird's eye view of the interior of the parlor and several other rooms. Why were they keeping such a close eye on the family? Was the husband a drinker or abusive? Was it a way of protecting their daughter and grandchildren or was it one more way that a controlling father tried to manage his daughter's life? We shall never know, unfortunately. Where the structure is silent, as is the history, we are left to construct meaning for ourselves and fill in the spaces with logical inferences.

Architecturally, this is a very good example of an Italianate home. It is three stories high, with a flat roof that is typical of the style. Additionally, there is filigree ironwork in several places, which is functional as well as ornamental. It serves to decorate the home and provide safety along the whistling walkway. The molding over the doorways and the roofs is also typical of the day and the style. I have included some pictures of the inside, as I was fortunate enough to be given a guided tour of the entire home prior to its renovation. I am very grateful for the information I was given and for my guide's excellent eye for historical detail.

THE PETITE HOUSE

When I first came upon the house I call "The Petite House," I had to stop and get out of my car to have a better look. It is without a doubt the tiniest little house I had ever seen. From the street, it looks more like a child's dollhouse, but up close, you can see that it is really rather roomy, it just happens to be very long. The owner, Kathy Davis, and I stood for quite awhile looking at the home the day that I came to shoot it and we stood speculating about its dimensions. She informed me that it is approximately thirty-five feet long and sixteen feet wide. She thinks it was probably added after the homes on either side of her were built, since it was so tiny. One interesting note is that the roof above the long, skinny window was constructed as if it were meant for someone to look out of it at some point. It should be noted, however, that it faces nothing except for the roof of the neighbor's house. It appears that the original contractor or the workers made a mistake when it was built, adding something that was never meant to be there at all. We also speculated, Ms. Davis and myself, about the possibility of the workers being "intemperate" at the time, which was quite plausible. While on lunch break, it was nothing to go somewhere to get a "bucket of beer" or send a local child to get one for you. My father verified that he did this many times for workers and they would give him a few pennies for his trouble. They would drink, eat, and then go right back to work. Could they have been drunk when they constructed the roof and by the time they realized their mistake, it was too late? We can only speculate!

There used to be stained glass over the wide part of the window and on the bottom, but Ms. Davis stated that it was her promise to the house that one day she would fix it like it originally was and put in stained glass. She has since created her own lovely stained glass to ornament and accentuate her interesting little piece of Butchertown history, keeping her promise as she said she would.

St. Joseph's Cathedral and School

With so many immigrants flooding the Butchertown area, the one main establishment that the area was lacking was a house of worship. Primarily populated with German immigrants and their families, they found it necessary to have a place to worship that was close to their homes. Prior to St. Joseph's construction, people had to travel quite a distance if they wanted to attend mass. This put families who were not wealthy enough to get to another parish into a very precarious situation. Who would baptize the children or minister last rites, if necessary? Where could one go to confess the sins of the night before? Even something as small as making it to mass on Holy days, which are days that the church really encourages people to attend, would have been a great burden for those who would readily go if they had a place close by. For those devout Catholics it would have been unbearable. Not having a home parish – a place where the bonds of family extended beyond mere flesh and blood and instead took the form of aligned spiritual beliefs and concerns – would have been unimaginable in home countries where every little berg had its own priest and church. People took joy in each birth and baptism and wept with each other at every death, whether related by blood or not. The church provided a sense of unity and every parishioner was part of the larger body of the church family. However, one can only do what is humanly possible and in Butchertown it was beginning to become apparent that something must be done about the situation. In 1864, it was decided that the Butchertown area needed its own parish, since it really wasn't right to have an entire portion of the population of an area sitting in their own unrepentant sin. However, the church that was to be

Notice the hooded molding over the doors and the Gothic Arch that is found both on the doors and repeated in the structure of the door molding.

The Fleur-de-lis symbol is carved here symbolizing the city of Louisville and her ties with France.

constructed was not intended only for the German speaking Catholics who lived in this area, even though that was a primary consideration. From the earliest plans it was intended for the German and Irish populations in the area. The amalgamated congregation of Germans and Irish lasted from 1865 when the cornerstone was laid until approximately 1876-77. It was at this time that the English speaking Irish were given their own parish at the corner of Washington and Buchanan Streets, which was called Blessed Sacrament. However, at its closing, many parishioners of Blessed Sacrament returned to worship as members of St. Joseph's once again. Of all the parishes in Louisville – all seventy-nine of them as a matter of fact – St. Joseph's is the ninth oldest. During the 1937 flood, many of the homes around the area were completely devastated and St. Joseph's School and parish served as both a place of refuge and respite for many local families.

The architecture of the church is Gothic Revival and was designed by architect A. Druiding in 1883. Prior to this construction, the building was a small unassuming house of worship and one that lacked the stone ornamentation and exquisite stained glass that can be seen today. The families who still worship at St. Joseph's parish have long histories there. One family, that of Mrs. Ellen Marie Jaggers, who is the director and manager of the St. Joseph Preschool, has been at that parish and in the area for so many generations that the altar that is used at each service is the original one that her great, great grandfather carved for the church. Happy to give back to the parish that gave them so much, the local residents rally around the church every time it sponsors an event, capturing and honoring the spirit of true community in which it was founded.

As noted by St. Joseph architectural historian Roy Hampton, "Most of St. Joseph's is in French Gothic introduced in the basic elements of Gothic Architecture: the pointed arch which can be found above many of the windows of St. Joseph's; the rose window, a large, round window with tracery that radiates outward, as seen on the church's (sic) façade; the vaulted ceiling, an arched ceiling with bays and recesses; and the flying buttress, a column connected to the building's wall by an arch, used to help support St. Joseph's ceiling because it is built of plaster and wood, rather than the heavy stone used to build the ceilings of medieval churches. St. Joseph's also contains elements of the German Gothic Style, which is characterized by heavy ornamentation and an emphasis on height. The three wooden altars of St. Joseph's, with their slender spires and elaborate tracery, all highlighted in gold leaf, are an excellent example of the German Gothic Style."[7]

Frontal view of St. Joseph's as seen from the steps.

Chapter Three:
Portland
& the Marine District

We cannot help the natural disasters that come our way and rob us of our historical landmarks and regional treasures. Tornadoes, fires, floods, and general disrepair have plagued the Portland district, a once thriving, beautiful place that served the transportation needs of people on both sides of the Ohio River. As cities do, however, when disasters befall specific areas of town and there is not enough revenue to fix the problems, the places become run-down shadows of their former greatness. Such is the case with the Portland district. Through the years, circumstances such as the 1937 flood and the 1974 tornado caused immense destruction and it has only been within the past ten years that the Urban Renewal Project and concerned residents of Portland have taken a stand on the preservation of this historically bountiful place.

If traveling in the city or through it, it is easy to overlook this treasure trove of architectural goodies. However, this district is not only the oldest in the city, but also has some of the most interesting stories in our city. Historically, Portland was a stopping place for boats that would travel up and down the Ohio River. The Falls of the Ohio, a natural barrier for boats, would make this stop-off a very profitable place for tavern owners and keepers, like our own legendary "Kentucky Giant" Big Jim Porter. James D. Porter, or "Big Jim" as he was known, plays an important role in the history of both Louisville and Portland, as he was somewhat of a celebrity at home and abroad. Though growing at a normal, if not slow pace during the first fourteen years of his life, Jim hit a growth spurt unlike any other boy around him. He began to grow and grow, until he stopped growing at 7'8". The span of his hand was thirteen inches long and it was rumored that he once carried a small girl across a street in the palm of his hand. His great stature attracted the likes of both PT Barnum, the great showman of circus fame, and renowned author, Charles Dickens, who met Porter personally. Barnum, of course, wanted Big Jim for his show, which Porter politely declined, choosing instead to continue to run his tavern and serve the guests who traveled up and down the Ohio River. Presumably suffering from a malady known as Gigantism, it's likely that a tumor on Porter's pituitary gland caused the enormous growth spurt and his incredible stature. His walking stick was over four feet long. His sword was five feet and his rifle, nicknamed "The Little Rifle" for comic effect, was over eight feet long. At the time of his death, his coffin was over nine feet long and was on display in Cave Hill Cemetery in Louisville. As most things do, it fell into disrepair and disintegrated, leaving nothing more than the stone marker that bears Big Jim's name and brags that he wasn't 7"8' — but that he was actually an inch shorter than he claimed. He came to represent a very proud segment of the

local population—those who earned their livings and lived well because of their own desire to succeed. He earned a reputation as a man to be reckoned with not only because of his immense stature but also because of his entrepreneurial spirit. Today, the only local tavern that bears his name is, ironically enough, not even located in Portland, but in the East End near Frankfort Avenue and Grinstead Drive. Big Jim, like many other residents, saw a need in the area and proceeded to fill it. Portland was awash with businesses that catered to the travelers on the boats coming up and down the river. The passengers would have to stop in Portland, disembark, and then board another boat on the other side of the Falls. This port, like most, meant money for the people who owned the local taverns, shops, and boarding houses.

While all the historical information is riveting and gives most of us who have ties to the area great pride, going there is a completely different experience. The stately homes that were once testaments to the optimism of the inhabitants now lie in states of disrepair due to circumstances beyond the control of those who live there. Once a thriving district, Portland has become synonymous with poverty, gang violence, and crime. In recent years, there has been a renewed effort to restore this once magnificent district to a modicum of its former glory, or at least a reasonable facsimile. The refurbishment of the Portland Marine Hospital, which all the locals swear is haunted by the ghosts of former patients and Civil War soldiers, has been a local project, one that residents and officials hope will bring a renewed sense of vitality to the area. One of seven original marine hospitals that the Federal government opened to treat sailors who would become ill on the trip up the Ohio, it was the last one to be shut down, earning it a spot on the

Historical Register. Officially shut down due to disrepair and flooding, locals say that if you look at just the right time, you can still see the sailors peering out the windows of the second floor, possibly gazing toward the river they love.

I have spoken with the current curator and he assured me that the Marine Hospital is most definitely NOT haunted. Many of the stories of people hearing whistling and seeing people lurking in the windows were fabricated by attention seekers or people who had no interest in the preservation of the landmark. He recalled that one person had come in, reporting that mysterious whistling had been heard in the corridors. Laughing, he stated that workmen had been there all afternoon and it was the janitor whom they had heard. He whistled constantly and was in the building at the time. The Marine Hospital is a true architectural wonder, retaining much of the original structure. The cupola is true to the way it would have been originally, even though it was redone in the reconstruction. When the windows were opened, the "sick air" from the other floors would be sucked up and out through the windows in the cupola, a unique and quite brilliant design. I was certainly impressed with the interior and the renovation efforts and know that upon completion, this magnificent building will once again be the crowning jewel of the Portland area.

SQUIRE JACOB EARICK HOUSE

One would never guess that the dilapidated structure that barely stands by itself at 719 North 34th Street is one of the two oldest homes in the city. It is eerie to walk up the stone steps that lead to the original structure, as you realize that a place once thriving with life and abundance is now silent. The jasmine that blooms on the chain link fence is heavy and fragrant, almost inviting someone to come sit on the porch. There is a stark contrast between the floral invitation and the restoration committee's obvious desire to keep vagrants and vandals away. A large chain link fence surrounds the home for reasons of security and safety, while the Portland Museum makes necessary restorative changes to the original structure. But what of the people, the original owners? We know from existing writings that there was a wife and some daughters. We know that they had to live on the top level as a family while many of the prisoners who were awaiting trial were kept below, in the basement. One can only imagine the horrors of what the young daughters had to endure, as the prisoners below were very likely by no means a quiet group. Yet, at the beginning of a nation, there are discomforts that had to be endured and this was one of them, I suppose. The house would have been a real sight to behold when first constructed, too. From where the house is located, Squire Jacob Earick would have been able to have a beautiful view of the river. The records reveal that the Earick House was used to try petty criminals and that they would be held in the basement, as it served as a make-shift jail. Yet, more interesting to me was the story that one of the main supporting beams in the basement of the house was actually a mast that was taken from a boat that had wrecked on the Falls of the Ohio. Additionally, the Squire Jacob Earick House was reported to be an important stop for slaves traveling on the Underground Railroad. Legend has it that the basement also served as a passageway to the river and that there was a special passage that led straight to the water. Unfortunately, the 1937 flood rendered it impossible for that fact to be checked, as the passageway caved in upon itself and is, even today, impassable. But, I think it is both ironic and interesting to note that one special residence, and specifically the basement of that residence, held both imprisonment and freedom for many. This was the story that I spoke about with a representative of the Portland Museum. It is unfortunate that the story I would have loved to believe was true, namely that the home was a passage for freedom for runaway slaves, was made up. Not certain where the story originated, the representative did verify that it was not true.

So what type of style would we characterize the Earick house? It is really too early for many of the styles listed in the first chapter, yet the scalloping around the edges of the roof and the front porch would lead me to call it an early form of Queen Anne. However, the internal construction is actually of more interest than the outside. Earick House is an example of a "timber framed" house, which is very different than the stick built houses of the later 1800s. A timber framed home was an exemplification of the skill of the builder and testified to his craftsmanship. A timber-framed house traditionally uses no nails to hold the frame together, instead using pegs to join the beams.

The Squire Jacob Earick House is believed to have been built between 1800 and 1820.

HOLLAND TAX HOUSE

When I first drove past the Holland Tax House, I could not believe that such a beautiful structure had been left to ruin and fall to the ground. One of the oldest, most stately structures in the city, I immediately fell in love with it, even in its present, fire-ravaged condition. I attempted to research the home, but even a search of the address turned up almost no information. What I did find was that the gorgeous mansion was originally owned by the Ouerbacker family and was designed by local architect, Arthur Loomis. Frank Samuel Ouerbacker, known commonly as Samuel Ouerbacker, was born in 1841 in Leavenworth, Indiana. He moved to Louisville, where he married Helen Gilmore, who was the daughter of a wealthy steamboat captain,

Even burned out and left to fall to the ground, the Holland Tax House stands as a regal reminder of the wealth and glory of its former days. It also serves as a visual reminder that unless the community cares enough to preserve its history, we can expect only more of this through the years.

Holland Income Tax House still stands due to the durability of the stone structure. Even a massive fire could not bring this house to the ground.

Alexander Gilmore. Ouerbacker began his own coffee roasting and importing business and became extremely wealthy, according to some sources. After the Ouerbacker's left the premisies, it was occupied by the former pastor of the African Methodist Episcopal Zion Church, the Rev. George C. Clement. He had possession of the home in the 1920s and 1930s and at one point during World War II, the mansion housed soldiers who needed rooms. The home was used as a tax preparation service until the city of Louisville took possession of it due to unpaid taxes. At the time of the fire, which started in the early evening hours of July 10, 2006, the house was on the Louisville Historical Society's list of ten most endangered homes. The cause of the fire was arson and had been set in the middle of the house. I could only peer between chain links of the fence, but I could see that the backyard and former garden area was at one time a lovely place to behold. The corner turret once faced out on the side garden and a person would have been able to sit there and still have a nice, but protected, view of the city street and those who walked past. It is a sad shame that no one has the funds to restore such a stately residence and that year after year it continues to fall further into ruins. The Richardsonian Romanesque style home sits directly across from one of the oldest cemeteries in the city. Many of the original inhabitants of this area lie buried in that cemetery, which has recently undergone preservation and renovation to the exterior walls. The Holland House, however, has not had that much luck. When I spoke to city officials and asked them about renovating it or possibly finding grant money to turn the home into some sort of museum for the area or a place where the youth of the city could have an after school program dedicated to the study of the Arts and Humanities, the person handling the house was more than willing to entertain any reasonable proposal. However, the funding necessary to bring the house back up to code so that it would be a safe place for anyone to live and work is astronomical and no one can come up with enough grants to restore this home. According to neighbors, the fact that the home was a fire hazard did not stop local hooligans from coming in after dark and ransacking whatever they could find in the home worth selling. They would come in and carry out entire fireplace mantels, door molding, and light fixtures that were all over a hundred years old. In order to do restorative justice to this home, it would have to be renovated by someone schooled in historic preservation. Unfortunately, very few contractors are willing to undertake such a feat. The Holland Tax House, as it is locally known, sits much the way it has for years—abandoned. It is my hope that someone will be able to restore it and use it for the betterment of a community that, like the Holland House, has been overlooked and under cared for through the decades. For me, the Holland Tax House has become a metaphor for the entire Portland area. Standing tall, even in the midst of destruction, the house symbolizes the endurance of an entire area of town that neither floods, nor tornadoes, nor fire can destroy. It is the spirit of the community embodied in one structure and it's my sincere hope that it will continue to survive until someone has the ability and the means to help it out of its present condition. Like those who live in the area, the home waits for the city to take an interest in a place that people simply overlook as they pass by on their way to other places, pretending that the need isn't there or that it's not their problem to deal with. Until attitudes change and people of our city reassess their priorities, both the neighborhood and the people who live there will continue to be a community that's ignored.

CHURCH OF OUR LADY (NOTRE DAME DU PORT)

When we think of the Portland area as it was in the early 1800s, we might be tempted to envision a city filled with rough trade and men who are looking to make it to the nearest house of ill repute as quickly as they can. Thinking of the rough and rowdy sailors getting off their boats to go drinking and brawling is both plausible and easily imagined. One has to stretch the imagination to think of these same men scurrying off their boats and hurrying through their chores in order to make it to mass so that they can perform their duties as altar boys! Yet, many of the sailors would do just this, making certain that while their bodies toiled, their souls were preserved and that they gave their church and their God the proper place in their lives. While the local taverns or mercantile were places of importance to the community and gave people a place to congregate and socialize, the most important establishment was the church. The church provided a place for people to gather, socialize, and worship, while it ministered to the immortal souls of the congregation. There were many functions that the church provided other than just daily mass and last rites. They provided relief for those in need, educational services, moral support, and unity in the community, while providing a bridge between the old life that immigrants left behind and their new one in America. Even if the language changed, and the customs were different, the one thing that remained the same was the church, its rites, and its foundation. No matter how wild the lifestyle, the church was there to absolve and hopefully reform even the rowdiest of behavior. The Church of Our Lady du Port, or Our Lady as it is known locally, was a haven for those seeking a place to worship on a stopover and a local parish to call home for those who chose to stay. It is a very unassuming church, one that does not speak of wealth or superfluous grandeur from the outside. Yet, the air that surrounds it is one of respectability, as it is one of the oldest churches in the city of Louisville. As most historians know, the surroundings of an area, its natural landforms and resources, will often drive the commerce, economy, and culture of a region. This is true of the Portland area, as well. The area was in desperate need of a house of worship in the early 1800s, as the other churches were far away from the river. The need for something is the driving force behind its acquisition and surrounding landforms, the Falls of the Ohio and the river itself were two factors in choosing the spot for Our Lady. People would be stopping and often staying in the area. It was an area that was doing well financially. Notre Dame du Port was established in 1839 as a more convenient parish for those who lived and passed through the Portland area. Our Lady is the third oldest parish in the Archdiocese of Louisville.

Our Lady was devastated by the great flood of 1937, the water being twenty feet deep at its deepest. The pictures of the interior of the building at that time show water over the pews and halfway up the large wooden doors. One of the Sisters recalls in her journal what the flood was like.

The following is an account from Sr. Mary Winifried, a Sister of Mercy and teacher at Our Lady School. At the time of the flood, she resided at St. Ann's Convent, located 2420 Portland Avenue.

January 24–31, 1937

The Sisters of St. Ann's became aware of the flood some time before Monday, January 18, when they noticed the waters from Bank Street flowing over to meet the waters from Portland Avenue. The currents met in St. Ann's yard and poured into the basement with a roar as deafening as that of Niagara Falls.

On Sunday, January 24, Mother advised the Sisters to leave. Thirty Sisters found shelter at the College, Presentation, and St. Helena's. The eight remaining, Sisters Mary Pierre, Mechtildes, Maria Teresa, Mary Thedla, Jean Catherine, Esther Maria, Winifred Ann, and Frances Lucille, remained to guard the Blessed Sacrament until it could be removed from the Chapel. Sr. Mary Pierre had been trying since Saturday to reach St. Cecilia's by phone for instructions about the Blessed Sacrament, but the telephone connection between the two places was dead. On Monday, Sister called Father Cotton, explaining her inability to reach St. Cecilia's. When she explained that it was Mother's wish that they leave, though they felt safe in remaining, Father advised that they wait a few days longer to see if the water would subside. He gave Sister permission to remove the Blessed Sacrament to the second floor, in the event water should come in on the first floor.

The eight Sisters settled down to remain comfortably at St. Ann's, with plenty of provisions, candle light, and part-time water and gas. Most of the days were spent watching the waters meet in the backyard, and huge army trucks going down Portland Avenue with provisions and returning with full loads of refugees. Soon the waters rose so high that nothing but motorboats, rowboats, and skiffs, in short, every conceivable kind of craft, was in use on Portland Avenue. The Sisters felt quite secure with the protection promised them by the fire department across the street. After the water reached a depth of seven feet and the firemen had to evacuate, the Sisters were left by the firemen under the protection of the Coast Guard and six able bodied men living next door to the Convent.

At about three o'clock on Wednesday, Mother Ann Sebastian phoned to tell Sr. Mary Pierre that she had been advised to have all the Sisters leave St. Ann's. Mother explained to Sr. Mary Pierre that Father Cotton had approved their leaving and had directed that the Sisters take the Blessed Sacrament with them and leave it at the nearest church. The relief agent at St. Joseph's Infirmary came on the line to say that a boat would call for the Sisters in from one to five hours. Within an hour, everything was ready and the Sisters were waiting for the boatmen, each Sister wearing an abundance of clothing. The Blessed Sacrament, in veils and encased in a small leather receptacle, was on the altar, with lighted candles. Here, the Sisters knelt in prayer (with interruption) until the call came at 7:30 p.m. that the boat was at the lower gate.

The water here was six feet deep. By means of a searchlight and calls from the Sisters, the men were directed how to reach the house, where the depth of the water was two and a half feet. The men told the Sister to get blankets and pillows to be used in the boat for protection and warmth. The gas was turned off; the house locked up. It was eight o'clock before the men began to row them out.

The Sisters had been praying for moonlight, and even though it was dark earlier in the evening, as they started, out the moon appeared. They directed their course up Portland Avenue one block, then turned over to Bank Street, proceeding up Bank to 20th. Passing the Good Shepherd Convent on Bank Street, they noticed the water was up to the top of the high wall surrounding the premises, with the Sisters marooned on the third floor. The current was very swift, especially at the intersections, and it was almost impossible for the oarsmen to keep to the middle of the street. They bumped into telegraph poles, traffic light standards, and even fences and houses. At one time, the boat tipped so much that it almost filled with water. One man steadied it by holding on to the street sign until his two companions had emptied out gallons of water. By that time, some of the Sisters were wet up to their knees.

Turning 20th Street to Rowan, the boat hit a pole with such force that it (the boat) was broken crosswise in two pieces. The smaller part sank and some of the Sisters floated with the current. Sr. Maria Teresa, who was carrying the Blessed Sacrament, was among those who were adrift. The others adrift were Sisters Mary Thelda, Mechtildes, Joan Catherine, and Winifred Ann. Sr. Mary Pierre was clinging to the floating suitcase and the end of the boat, while Sisters Esther Maria and Frances Lucille clung tightly with arms and legs to a pole. Sr. Mary Pierre could see that Sr. Maria Teresa was clasping the leather receptacle containing the Blessed Sacrament, holding it aloft until she was rescued, although she sank twice. They got those who were floating first, took them to a house and broke open a door in order to enter.

In the meantime, one of the other men had broken into another house and sheltered two Sisters there. When one of the oarsmen said to Sr. Frances Lucille, "Hold on tight, don't let go of me," Sister replied, "Man, I wouldn't let go of you for a million dollars." They soon had a fire, chairs having been broken up for fuel. Sisters Mary Pierre, Esther Maria, and Frances Lucille were the last to be rescued. When Sr. Mary Pierre was taken into the house, she found five Sisters praying before the Blessed Sacrament. Sr. Mary Winifred repeatedly broke in with "Lord, Let one of us live to tell the tale!"

Sr. Mary Pierre was immediately alarmed when she discovered that there were only six Sisters in the house to which she had been taken, and even though assured by a policeman that the other Sisters were in an adjacent house, she could not rest satisfied until all eight of them had been transported to another motor boat. This boat (a New York relief boat) had accidentally, and not in answer to repeated shouts and siren calls, come along. It was taking Dr. Bryan of the Brown Hotel on an urgent sick call, and fortunately, it was a government boat and well manned. It was so large that it could not come close to the house, so the Sisters were taken to it, one at a time, in small skiffs. The Sisters felt secure when they got into this boat. It was here that Sr. Mary Pierre held up her skirts so that she could navigate, and went around counting heads to satisfy herself that there were eight.

Sr. Mary Pierre's fears were again awakened when, on asking to be taken to St. Joseph's Infirmary, she was told that they would have to go to the City Hospital, the City Hall, or the Deaconess Hospital. Noticing Sister's hesitation, the men suggested the Good Shepherd Convent, and Sister gladly acquiesced. A young man aboard the boat, who had been marooned in the park all day awaiting transportation, knew the neighborhood and continued to call the names of the streets to the captain until they reached the 18th and Broadway relief station. Another man aboard, a Jew, warned those navigating the boat to be especially careful of Sr. Maria Teresa, as she was carrying "the Sacrament."

At the relief station, the Sisters were transferred to covered trucks. Sr. Mary Mechtildes, who seemed quite exhausted, was stretched out under covers on the floor of the truck. She had lost her cap and bonnet in the water. The doctor accompanied the Sisters to the Good Shepherd Convent and ordered that Sr. Mary Mechtildes be put to bed at once. The Blessed Sacrament was put away immediately upon arrival. It had been found intact. Deo Gratias! The other Sisters, with their heavy clinging, dripping clothes, stood around the stove to get warm and after being given hot drinks were taken to bed. Morning dawned, but the Sisters did not rise for prayers. The only clothing they had was drying out, so there was only one alternative. The Sisters of the Good Shepherd could not have been kinder; they exhausted themselves in providing for the Sisters and anticipated their every need.

On Sunday morning, word came that a truck or an ambulance would be sent for the Sisters, since the water was down, and that they were to be conveyed to St. Joseph's Infirmary. Here automobiles were to meet them and take them to Nazareth. The Sisters of the Good Shepherd bade them a most affectionate farewell and seemed greatly concerned about their safe passage to St. Joseph's. They reached the Infirmary at about 4:30 p.m., when an amusing scene followed. Their guide, an army man, entered with the Sisters, escorting them with the same rigid precision with which he had carried out previous orders given him under martial law. None of the Sisters standing by to greet the eight refugees was allowed to come near them, and the eight had been warned to speak to no one. For all the world, they looked like immigrants taken from Ellis Island. The Sisters were detained at the Infirmary only long enough to be greeted, given refreshments, and sent on their way rejoicing to Nazareth. Words are inadequate to describe the welcome these refugees received at Nazareth, the Motherhouse.[8]

The structure of Notre Dame du Port is not truly visible as a Gothic Revival styled church from the exterior view. You might be able to detect some aspects of the style in the arched windows and the steeply pitched roof. However, it is not until you step inside and see the buttresses and vaults that you become aware that the outside is deceiving as to the immense beauty of the building. This is most definitely Gothic Revival and is a pearl in the oyster of the Portland community, just waiting to be discovered. Notre Dame du Port, the Church of Our Lady, still stands today much as it did the in the mid 1800s, beckoning to all who could hear it bell to come and worship.

PORTLAND MARINE HOSPITAL

Few of the local landmarks in Portland are as well known nationally as the Portland Marine Hospital. When it was first constructed in 1845, it was one of seven marine hospitals that the Federal government commissioned to be built. Of the seven, the only one that remains standing is the one in

Louisville. The government realized the dangers that workers and sailors faced in their professions. Long-term exposure to the elements and inclement weather, diseases of the day, and injuries that were associated with malfunctioning or deficient equipment plagued numerous sailors. The Portland Marine Hospital served as a place where they could stop and be treated, rest and recuperate, eventually returning to their homes and families.

The website dedicated to the refurbishment of this Historic Landmark discusses who was eligible for services at the hospital when it states:

> The boatmen served by the hospital worked difficult and dangerous jobs. Injuries due to engine or boiler explosions, wrecks, collisions with river snags, and freight handling were common dangers. Exposure to extremes of temperature, from the sub-tropic heat of the Mississippi delta to frigid Great Lakes, claimed victims.
>
> Diseases affecting the boatmen included yellow fever, cholera, smallpox, and malaria. While docked in the rough port towns of the time, violence, alcoholism and social diseases sent many boatmen to the marine hospitals.
>
> In the early days, 20 cents a month was withheld from their salaries to pay the boatmen's share of their healthcare in marine hospitals, with the federal government also providing support. This was the first example of pre-paid health insurance in American history.
>
> All classifications of river workers were eligible for treatment. Every mariner, including pilots, captains, cooks, pursers, engineers, stevedores, roustabouts and deckhands, were eligible for treatment and care. It is estimated that one-third of the patients were African-Americans.
>
> The Marine Hospital Service was the genesis of America's modern health care system and is responsible for major improvements in research, hygiene, and science-based medical treatment.[9]

The hospital was designed to be exactly where it was — strategically placed between the Portland and Louisville wharfs, with the hope that the sailors would be encouraged and strengthened by the sight of the river, the love of many of their lives. The 1800s were a time of great turmoil, even for those choosing to remain neutral during the War Between the States. Kentucky chose to stay out of the war officially, but lent itself to helping both sides by giving protection and medical treatment to the troops from both the North and the South.

The Marine Hospital was constructed in 1845 and is considered a Greek Revival building. Known as one of the finest examples of antebellum architecture in the city, the hospital is symmetrical and balanced, perhaps structured this way to create a sense of harmony and well being in order to benefit those who were ailing and those who were on the mend. The cupola atop the roof draws attention to the fact that it would give a nice amount of natural light to the interior of the building.

WESTERN MIDDLE SCHOOL

Standing like a fortress at 22nd and Main Street in Louisville, Western Middle School is both an architectural gem and a functional building. Out of the 145 schools in the Jefferson County School District, Western Middle was constructed to service the children of the Portland area. Many of the students are within walking distance of the three-story school building. While many changes have been made over the years, one thing hasn't changed — its families. Families who have made the Portland area home generation after generation will have many members that attended the school. My father attended Western Middle in the late 1940s and, when I took a teaching position there, he asked me if the old hardwood floors were still there. And, yes, after working there for some time, I realized that indeed the floors were still exactly where he said they were. Walking the same halls he once did gives me a concrete tie to both the school and this community and the families whose children attend Western feel that tie, as well. It served as a place for people to come when the 1937 flood rocked the riverside town. Serving the community whenever it needed them, Western also was a place of refuge during World War II.

Today, Western Middle School partners with the University of Louisville in a program call TCP Scholars. Students who are invited to participate in this program have set themselves apart academically and as future leaders. The University sends students to mentor to

Western Middle School is located at 2201 West Main Street.

these middle school students and, in the process, the partnership between the two institutions encourages students to internalize the fact that "college is for everyone." The leadership at both educational facilities is determined to provide university access for all students, thereby changing the culture of an entire district and the families who live there. By making education a top priority for the students, it encourages them to envision themselves as the leaders and university graduates of the future.

Western Middle stretches across a block and the structure is mostly brick and stone. It has battlements that run the length of the building, making it look like a medieval castle at the top. There are strong Gothic accents in the hooded moldings over the doors, but I would hesitate to call it a true Gothic Revival structure, although that argument could certainly be made.

Detail of the figure adorning the top of the St. James fountain.

Chapter Four:

OLD LOUISVILLE
& BELGRAVIA COURT

N ot just another historic district or pretty facade, Old Louisville stands out as one of the most interesting areas of town since it has achieved both local and national attention. Old Louisville is listed as the country's third largest district comprised almost solely of Victorian homes and it boasts one of the largest collections of original, intact stained glass within those homes. Sometimes referred to as Louisville's Oldest Subdivision, Old Louisville and St. James Court/Belgravia Court were originally land tracts made up of a thousand acres. These were sold or given to wealthy Virginians after the Revolutionary War, as Kentucky was so closely linked with the Virginia Territories prior to it becoming its own "state" (Commonwealth) in June of 1792. It was a little over a hundred years later that the area had evolved and blossomed into one of the grandest examples of what is commonly called "Victorian" architecture in the entire country. Marked by one of the most beautiful fountains in the city, the St. James Court Fountain acts as the unofficial landmark of the area.

One cannot list the homes of Belgravia Court with the homes in all the other areas of the city. It simply would not do justice to these places that deserve to be show-cased in their own right. The homes of Belgravia Court do stand out as constant reminders of the importance of architectural preservation. This

St. James Fountain was originally made in Brooklyn, New York and placed in St. James Court in 1892. However, the iron of the Fountain deteriorated through the years, so it was disassembled and re-cast as the bronze one that stands there today. Notice the intricate railing that surrounds the fountain. It was originally the railing that went around the box seats of the Strand Theatre.

Detail of the underside of the fountain.

historic district is worth the time and the interest that it would take to walk the tree lined streets, breathing in the beauty and elegance of a by-gone era. As a Louisvillian, I had long known the streets, passed by the fountain more times than I can count, and actually lived in one of the old Victorian mansions in my college days. My friends and I used to sit on the grass, talking of poetry, Keats, Shelley, and Byron, pretending that we were artists and Bohemians instead of middle-class college kids. As an adult, I find it interesting that even in college, my friends and I were drawn to the same neighborhood that continues to draw those who love history and the architecture of our city. Belgravia Court and Old Louisville helped put Louisville on the map after the Civil War. Belgravia Court, and forty-five acres in the general area, hosted the Southern Exposition of 1883, which was opened by then President Chester A. Arthur.

The Southern Exposition was a series of World Fairs that were to last one hundred days and showcase the highlights of the emerging industrial and technological advances. The incandescent light bulb, courtesy of Mr. Thomas Edison, was widely used at the Southern Exposition and Louisville is credited with firing up the most incandescent lights at one time. Those who witnessed the event, I am told, say that the entire area was aglow with

Two views of the Magnolia Belle House in St. James Court.

light, but that it was considered more of a novelty than a realistic invention that would be used in almost every home. I find it pleasingly ironic that Mr. Edison, who had lived not even ten miles away, and who had been fired from his job in Louisville sixteen years prior, saw the fruits of his labor unfold in a magnificent display of incandescent light at the Southern Exposition. It was his dream, which had come full circle.

A view of St. James Court.

The homes on Belgravia Court are among the most impressive in the entire area. Not only aesthetically pleasing, the stories that accompany them are as amazing as the residents who live there, preserving the history through their love of, and for, the structure. As I walked the other night, shooting last minute pictures as the light quickly faded behind me, I found a rather interesting home that I had overlooked previously. While not the most ornate or typically styled home in the area, there was an interesting air about it and it made me stop and linger for a second and then a third look. It was yellow and, as much as I could tell, was somewhat of a Queen Anne style. It had a porch and some gingerbread, and it was only upon closer examination that I found there were two gentlemen sitting on the screened porch, observing me observing their home. As I approached and asked for permission to use their home for my book, a request that can often make people uncomfortable to say the least, they graciously invited me to come up and talk for awhile. It never ceases to amaze me at the treasure trove of stories that are lying around our city, just waiting to be uncovered. It just so happened that while this home was indeed a Queen Anne style, what made it interesting was the litany of people who had lived there previously. It had been home to Michael Grossman, a premier architect in the city of Louisville. Oscar winner Kathy Bates, a native Louisvillian, had also lived there in the 1980s. Beverly Sills had lived there and performed a concert on the grassy common area in front of the house. She had done this for a man who lay dying in the home and could not make it out to hear her play. Yet, most interesting is the fact that I stood in the screened in porch area where Pulitzer-prize winning playwright Marsha Norman wrote her play "Night Mother"! It is such a pleasure to know that such a lovely, warm home has such great stories to go with it and both gentlemen have gone to great lengths to restore it to a level of elegance and refinement that may not have been there originally.

FERGUSON MANSION/FILSON HISTORICAL SOCIETY

While Old Louisville's premier museum, extensive library, and private collection of historical memorabilia might go unnoticed if one drives too quickly down 4th Street, overlooking the headquarters for the Filson Club would be a shame. When I first was introduced to the landmark and historic home, it was for a professional development for teachers called, "Teachers as Scholars." The Filson Club promotes the development and continuing education for teachers of all content areas, not just history. Upon walking into the establishment, my breath was taken away by the beauty and elegance that must be a mere shadow compared to the glory days when this house was a thriving home. Completed in 1905, the Ferguson Mansion, as it was then known, was the most expensive home in Louisville. Designed by architect William J. Dodd, the Beaux Arts styled home exceeded $100,000 at its completion, making this dwelling a living, breathing example of American affluence living the American Dream. Unlike many of the aristocrats of the Old South who were willing to rest on the accomplishments and laurels of their patriarchs, Mr. Edwin Hite Ferguson spent the better part of his life forging his own businesses that were based on the sales of cottonseed-oil and later, soap. He had the good fortune to be born into a family who already owned an established and prosperous tobacco business, yet he, as many Americans choose to do, wanted to make his own fortune in the world. As president of the Louisville Soap Company, he needed a place that spoke of his prosperity and hard work, even if he kept silent for the rest of his life and thus was this beautiful home constructed. Yet, if the profession of the man who bought the Ferguson Mansion in 1926 when Mr. Ferguson sold it reflects any moral to the story of this structure, it would be that nothing lasts forever. Mr. C. D. Pearson, a local funeral director whose family has been in Louisville for over 150 years, bought it and converted the lower floors of the brick and limestone home into a funeral parlor, while continuing to preserve the upper floors as a private home. While Mr. Pearson modified the home to suit his needs and his tastes, it remained mostly unchanged structurally, which is where the Filson Historical Society found it in 1984. The members of the Filson Historical Society are respected throughout Louisville as the "resident experts" regarding our city and much of Kentucky. They study and procure many primary sources of information that shine light on areas of our state and city's history, which might have been buried otherwise. Housing documents that belonged to the Lewis and Clark expedition and a letter written by General George Rogers Clark, the Filson Club gives back to the Louisville community by allowing visitors and schools to come in and view their private collections. Additionally, they give seminars, teaching educators to incorporate local history into the core content and curriculum of the district.

The Filson Historical Society is now housed in what was once the most expensive private dwelling in the city.

THE CONRAD CALDWELL HOUSE

There are always exceptions. Exceptional minds, exceptional beauties, exceptional brilliance. The Conrad-Caldwell House is one of those exceptional places that stands apart from the rest of the crowd and makes those who pass it take notice, whether they want to or not. The heavy stone structure speaks of endurance and the grandeur that one associates with old, European structures. While Europeans built their structures to last for centuries, against invaders and the elements, one can only imagine that Mr. Conrad must have had it in mind that his home must outlast the nouveau riche of the latter 1900s, making a statement to the rest of the community. When I first laid eyes on the home, I was only about 18. My friends and I had walked from the University to Central Park to catch a free production of Shakespeare. While I cannot tell you the play that night, I can tell you that I was so mesmerized with the beauty of the Conrad-Caldwell House that even as an adult, it still fills me with awe. It is often referred to as "Conrad's Castle" due to the heavy stone, gargoyles, and fleur-de-lis, which adorn the exterior. Originally built in 1892 for Theophilus Conrad, who made his fortune in the tanning business, the home was built, according to the statistics from the Caldwell House, for $75,000. The Conrads sold the home in 1905 to the Caldwells until it was sold some thirty-five years later to the Rose Anna Hughes Presbyterian Nursing Home. It remained a home for the elderly until 1987 when the St. James Court Association bought it, restoring it to all the beauty and grandeur of its heyday.

A full image of Conrad Caldwell House as seen from the street.

The gargoyles look more like fish out of water to me, but their presence is none the less impressive. Notice how the stone is intricately carved into a pattern that almost resembles a Celtic Knot.

Conrad's Castle is a Richardsonian mansion that lives up to every expectation that Mr. Richardson would have had for such a structure. The heavy, rough stone has an uncut appearance and gives the structure real weight. It is immediately noticed and stands out among all the other homes of the area. The home sports heavy ornamentation in some areas and has a nice, open balustrade upon which the family might have sat in the summer. It is a breath-taking example of Richardsonian Romanesque and continues to be an architectural favorite for everyone who visits there.

THE PINK PALACE

The home that stands at 1473 Belgravia Court cannot be missed. Literally. Aptly nicknamed "The Pink Palace," it has been characterized by some as being "Chateauesque." The most obvious indication of this would be the high, pointed tower and the sharply gabled dormers. However, it really strikes me as more of a refined Queen Anne Style, with its sprawling front porch and "fish scale" shingles on the tower. Yet, no matter what one would call it, it certainly is a beautiful representation of this area. Sitting right on the end of one court and backing up to another, the color alone sets this home apart as something special and with that usually comes a good story. Most up-scale neighborhoods and their residents like to have a place to go where they can talk and socialize without having to leave the comfort of their own area of town. It is not surprising that the residents of St. James Court decided to make this grand home the official site of what was known as the "St. James Club," also known locally as "The Casino." While I could not find very much information on whether or not an actual casino was run inside the home, it would not surprise me if it were more of a place where men went to play cards, smoke cigars, and generally avoid their wives. In our kinder and gentler terms, I would like to think of it more as a residential respite for the domestically challenged than a gaming house. Yet, nothing good lasts forever and it was not long before the times they were a'changin'. Given the social stigma of drinking and gambling in the late 1800s, well-intentioned do-gooders decided that the best thing would be to buy it and set the neighborhood on the straight and narrow. Bought in 1910 by the Women's Christian Temperance Movement, they changed the home from its original brick/terra cotta color to a softer pink. I am sure the color change was meant to make both a statement about future use and as a distancing device to separate it from its intemperate past.

The Pink Palace.

402 BELGRAVIA COURT

While I do not agree with every identification of the architecture of this area of town, I must say that this home, built in 1897, is very much French Renaissance Chateauesque. Most would say that this home is a little late for French Renaissance, as it waned in or around 1890. Additionally, it lacks the round turrets and towers that one would associate with this style. However, it does have high, rectangular windows that are elaborate and grouped in twos and threes, which is also typical of the style. No matter how one would identify the architectural style, it is a home that is unlike any other on the court. The winding front staircase that leads up to the front door, also acts as a roof to a lower level door, which is guarded by a wrought iron

gate. The molded frame over the front door accentuates its symmetry and the simplicity of design, while focusing on the intricacy of its ornate detail and scrollwork. Louisville's own Fleur-de-lis is worked throughout the moldings and is also present in the stained glass.

Notice the fleur-de-lis present as a relief and echoed in the stained glass on these private residences.

Another Chateauesque style home on 3rd Street. Notice the elaborate carvings and detail above the windows and on the roof.

PRESENTATION ACADEMY

The name of Presentation Academy has been associated with the highest excellence in education and female instruction. The red brick building stands as an example of endurance, one of the many character traits instilled into the young women who attend. Started in 1831 by Mother Catherine Spalding, the first superior of the Sisters of Charity of Nazareth, the college preparatory school is the oldest, continuously running school in Louisville. Pres (pronounced "Prez"), as it is known locally, is situated right next to the university that honors Mother Spalding's contributions to the Louisville community by gracing it with her name. Born in Charles County, Maryland in 1793, young Catherine was brought to Kentucky by her mother, a widow. Some time later, her mother died, leaving Catherine orphaned and alone. She was raised by relatives until taking holy orders in 1812. Education, which was near and dear to her heart, took priority in her life and she founded many schools, hospitals, and one charity that was especially close to her heart, St. Vincent's Orphanage. Presentation continues to honor the tradition of holding their students to the highest of standards and in doing so, preserves a legacy. The structure itself is classified as Richardsonian Romanesque, a popular architectural style in the Old Louisville district. The high, rounded tower was constructed by D. X. Murphy, the same architect who designed the twin spires for Churchill Downs. Presentation is more than just a local landmark to the families who continue to support its mission by sending their daughters. Presentation Academy endures as a testament to one lady's belief that education and the well being of others is a sacred responsibility that all community members should honor and encourage.

LAMPTON BAPTIST CHURCH

While I was not able to uncover much history of the Lampton Baptist Church, its architecture is worth a look. It is located on the National Register of Historic Places and is dated around 1900. The establishment used to be the First Christian Church and is located at 850 South Fourth Street. The building is Beaux Arts and it sits within walking distance of the Louisville Free Public Library and is directly across the street from Spalding University. Designed by architects McDonald and Dodd, the Beaux Arts style is characterized by the Neo-Classical look. The cupola on top is an excellent example of how this device can be used to let in natural light so that the interior is illuminated. The Corinthian style capitals on the columns

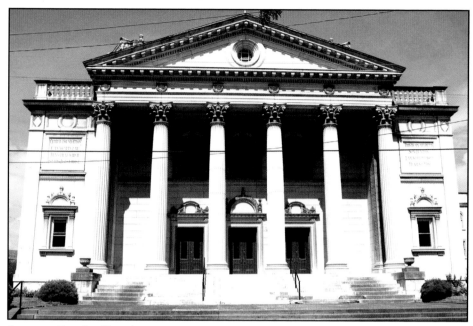

Lampton Baptist Church.

are extremely detailed and excellent examples of how stone was carved to look like acanthus leaves.

LOUISVILLE FREE PUBLIC LIBRARY

Even though Louisville did not always have a free public library, there was always a place where great books of the past were accessible to the general

The interlocking chain of acanthus leaves and fleur-de-lis serve as visual reminders of classical studies, as well as our ties to our French heritage.

The Louisville Free Public Library

public. With Kentucky joining the Union in 1792, by 1816 we could boast our very own small, private book collection, which was housed in the Old Court House, but it could by no means be considered a "library." However, after many years of waiting and a very generous grant from humanitarian and philanthropist Andrew Carnegie, 1905 saw a great change in the structure of Louisville as workers began to construct the gorgeous Beaux Arts/Greek Revival building that now houses the Louisville Free Public Library. It is interestingly noted that the Library did very well as a business and prospered so much that other buildings were added in different parts of the city. While the main branch of the library flourished, it was not the only branch opened during that time. Segregation ran rampant in the state, dictating to the African American population not only where they could eat, sit, or work, but also where they could read and check out books. It is cold comfort for those who remember those terrible days of injustice and prejudice, to be told that Louisville was progressive compared to other states in respect

Green Man

Detail of dentil molding under the roof, acanthus swirls, and cherubs/Italianesque puti

to the library system. While other states were ignoring the basic rights of African Americans to even read or sit in a library, Kentucky did provide this for its large African American demographic and that is something that should be acknowledged. The Western Branch of the Louisville Free Public Library was the first library in the entire United States to be chartered solely for the African American population. While this was a major milestone for Louisville given the time and the events of the day, it still must be noted that this branch was opened to keep people from the West End of Louisville from infiltrating into the white neighborhoods of the East End. Linking our collective cultural experience and history of our city to the places that house collections of rare and ancient manuscripts is a positive move. However, we must still keep this in context

Satyr face above an outdoor alcove

by realizing that the buildings themselves serve as reminders – to the entire population of our city – of the damage that ignorance can cause. Sitting empty today, one specific library reminds any who gazes upon it that only through knowledge can justice and equality ever blossom and grow. Keeping such buildings around instead of razing them makes a much stronger statement about the cultural growth we have experienced and the commitment that we, the citizens, have to the diversity and differences that makes Louisville such a wonderful city.

Beaux Arts structures will often hearken back to Greek and Roman Revivalist styles, sporting giant columns and intricate carvings. The titanic columns are separated into three basic parts, the base, the capital, and the entablature. The lower part of the column is the base, the upper is the capital, and the area that is supported by the entire column is called the entablature. The Louisville Public Library's columns are adorned with simple, yet elegant Ionic capitals. It is worth noting that the volute, or scroll-like carvings characterize the Ionic capitals, as the main focus of decoration. Additionally, the gargoyles-que faces that are strategically placed around the building are worth a second glance. At first grotesque, one begins to notice that they are more like satyrs or "green men" than gargoyles. The character of the building begins to emerge, as one begins to understand the representations on the outside of the building could be symbolic reflections of what was on the inside. As a public building, the classical structure and architecture would have bequeathed a certain amount of respectability and grandeur to the facility. However, the exterior embellishments would lead one to infer that while this was a place of serious study and scholarship, it was also the birth of a haven where those who wish to pursue knowledge in any area, could go. Collections of works are housed there. Information on the arts, sciences, philosophy, etc was all part and parcel of what the library represented. Not just a place to check out a book or two, the library symbolized a place where all were welcome to come and learn. The architect appears to have personalized the library to Louisville, also. The intricate fleur-de-lis carvings around the front and sides of the building remind us of where we came from and who we are today.

WALNUT STREET BAPTIST CHURCH

Walnut Street Baptist Church did not exist in the beginning as it does today, as is the case with many churches. Walnut Street traces its start from

Walnut Street Baptist Church as it looks today.

Notice how the large stone tower is covered in crockets. Crockets are stone spurs that project like miniature hooks and are found at regular intervals on the towers and spires of Gothic structures.

1815 and the First Baptist Church of Louisville. First Baptist began in 1815 and the Second Baptist Church of Louisville was founded in 1838. The two churches realized that merging in a central location, namely the up and coming district of the wealthy elite, would be advantageous. In 1848, both churches merged together to form what is known today as Walnut Street Baptist Church. Even though it has not resided on Walnut Street since 1902, it still retains the name. The architecture of the church has been described as "stone Gothic," which I find interesting since the outside is not stone, but rather, stucco made to look like stone. It is undeniably one of the most recognizable and beautiful churches in Louisville. What started out as a merging of congregations many years ago has grown into a thriving congregation that continues to reach out and give back to its community. Walnut Street Baptist Church is a gorgeous example of Gothic style architecture. Its stonework is breathtaking and its stained glass rivals many of the cathedrals in Louisville. It did not begin as the elegant and opulent structure that it is today, but thanks to the vision of the architect and the vision of the congregation, it stands today as a marker on the historic register.

UNIVERSITY OF LOUISVILLE

I would be remiss if I neglected to put a page in *Louisville Architectural Tours* for the University that inspired my love of the Humanities and specifically, the buildings in my city. Chartered in 1798 as the Jefferson Seminary, the University of Louisville has been serving the scholarly and educational needs of our community ever since. Bringing students together from over 116 countries around the world and from all fifty states, the university boasts top honors in many of its schools, such as Brandeis School of Law and Speed School of Engineering. Grawemeyer Hall, which is now an administrative building, was modeled after the Rotunda, designed by

University of Louisville Campus.

Rodin's "The Thinker" — Grawemeyer Hall.

Thomas Jefferson for the University of Virginia. The only other structure like this can be found on the campus of the Southern Methodist University. While Grawemeyer Hall is relatively new, constructed in 1927, it takes one back to the Jeffersonian days when construction of such a building would have been about "the authority of nature and the power of reason." Jefferson's design gives a beautiful dome to Grawemeyer Hall, but it is

Grawemeyer Hall.

the statue of Auguste Rodin's "The Thinker" that takes your breath away. Purportedly supervised by the artist himself, this bronze statue reminds students and visitors alike of the purpose of the campus — using one's mind and in doing so, bettering the world around them.

Louis Brandeis School of Law.

Chapter Five:

FRANKFORT AVENUE

I might be a little biased when it comes to recording the beautiful homes and buildings of this area of town, because I spent the better part of my childhood wandering the familiar sidewalks. The old homes speak volumes about the families who used the area as "summer lodgings" and would come to the "suburbs" from the inner city. The history of the Crescent Hill area dates backs to the late 1700s according to the Crescent Hill Community Council. The railroad opened up many possibilities and around 1853, Crescent Hill constructed a Fairground that held expositions and fairs for many years. The area continued to thrive and prosper, drawing many families there. I have credited the Crescent Hill Public Library for instilling in me a voracious appetite for and a love of books. Since it was right behind my house, I could, and did, often walk to the library. Living as an only child, as my siblings were both in their teens when I was born, there are only so many ways to entertain oneself. I was luckier than most children as I had a place to go, a place to call my own. The library provided a world of escape for a child who dreamed of traveling abroad and had no other children to talk to or play with. Growing up in an older neighborhood that had very few families with children my age, the library was a place to go and there was always something exciting going on there. It was a place that opened up an entire world of possibilities and set me on a course for a career as a life long learner. Classified as Beaux Arts, the library stands on Frankfort Avenue much the way that it did when it was first built in 1908. The Carnegie Endowment had made provisions for nine libraries in the Louisville area and through that kind donation, the Crescent Hill Public Library was the first one built. The large stone pillars and enormous pediment give those who enter the building the reassuring feeling that inside is a place where ideas and the books that house them, are still revered and protected inside an establishment that can withstand the elements. In an area that is prone to severe tornado activity, that is a reassuring feeling. In 1974 a severe tornado outbreak damaged a large part of the Crescent Hill area, including our home. As the sky turned a sick, greenish gray color, we all knew that something was seriously wrong and that this was not your usual storm. My mother called for my brother, who blew her off as teenagers always do. She insisted and he came inside the house as my sister grabbed me and headed for the basement. We all crouched underneath the pool table as a freight train drove over the top of our house. At least, that was what it sounded like to a terrified four-year-old. As we waited to be able to come out, none of us would be able to imagine the extent of the damage to the area and many of its old historic homes and buildings. We emerged from the basement, halfway expecting to be greeted with Munchkins and the Lollipop Guild. It was a surreal experience, retrospectively speaking. As we gazed at the damage to our neighbor's homes and yards, we turned to look at our own home. Our front door had been ripped from the hinges and the suction of the tornado had torn our roof completely off. As I stood on the hundred-year-old tree that had been uprooted from our neighbor's yard and planted itself horizontally across ours, I walked and played on it, wishing that it could stay for a while. Categorized as an F4 tornado, the super storm killed two people and injured 207 as it tore through the area, but through all the damage, the library remained.

CRESCENT HILL BAPTIST CHURCH

As a child, I often drove past this building on my way to school, or rode my bicycle past it on my trek around the two block area that my parents had given me permission to go. Like most of us do when we look back, the child's perspective seems so small in comparison to the adult point of view. As a child, the two blocks I had permission circle might as well have been ten miles of rugged terrain, for the world was a much bigger place back then. To mark my turning point, the place that marked the invisible boundary separating safety from danger, was the church. My parents were certain that any further would spell disaster, so I complied, knowing that the huge establishment was both safety and obedience. However, as a little girl, the church was huge! It was as if I were looking at the Lincoln Monument from the perspective of an ant…a very tiny ant. Yet, even as I re-visit it today, I am awed by the sheer grandeur of the building and amazed by the elegance of the architecture. As I stand underneath the titanic columns, I am surprised that I still feel very small. However, it would not surprise me if the original architect had this exact feeling in mind for those whom he envisioned standing in my exact spot. What better way to emphasize

Crescent Hill Baptist Church

The actual building is much longer, but you can see the frieze at the top of the pediment, the Corinthian capitals, and the Italian style bell tower.

the enormity of the Creator and the tiny, finite world of the human being than to create a structure whose enormous proportions do exactly that? Anyone who stands beside the seemingly mile high columns who be remiss is they were not mindful that the intent of the designer was very likely to emphasize the strength and colossal omnipresence of the Designer.

No one really knows why some churches succeed and others are incorporated into others. Yet, the importance of a house of worship to a community cannot be measured in any quantitative terms. It provides for those in need, the poor and distraught, those who are suffering, or simply those who need a place to rest or obtain pastoral care and counseling. It cannot be denied, though, that people are still people and often cannot reconcile differences in personality or personality clashes. Conflicts that arise among individuals and differing opinions on logistical matters of business will set congregations at odds with one another. No matter what the reason, Crescent Hill Baptist Church began as an offshoot of Clifton Baptist Church in 1908, when member of the congregation decided that a church was needed in the growing Crescent Hill area. It was not until 1926, however, that the cornerstone of the building was laid and the architectural structure that is so impressive today was begun. The church can be categorized as Greek Revival, since is sports an extremely impressive portico, a porch or entryway that leads to the front of a building. Its columns support a roof, but there is also a colonnade, or walkway, under the roof structure, as well. The enormous columns have Corinthian capitals, which I had to examine closer to make sure they were truly Corinthian in style. The give away for me was the fact that the lower "leaves" at the base of the capital appear to be set in the "cup" of another set of leaves, giving it a stacked appearance. The top of the capital appears to have stone "foliage" and both of these lend themselves to the Corinthian style. One has to wonder if, when the architects laid the plans for the building, they ever considered another type of capital. After all, Corinth and Paul's letters to the Corinthians are important to the New Testament, so one has to wonder if choosing this style was also making a statement about becoming a New Testament church. As I discussed this possibility with my husband, he asked what many people might ask. So, how does a Corinthian capital indicate a statement about or tie the building's capital to the Bible? My reply was: Well, there is no letter to the Dorians or to the Ionians. However, there is a letter to the Corinthians, so there is the tie. I include this because if he asks this question, others may too. Yet, it must be noted that the connection between the two is pure speculation, and the architectural coincidence could be merely happenstance. But, if it is not and it was planned this way, the founders, planners, and designers were extremely clever, indeed. I could not find very much information on the frieze that adorns the pediment. The pediment is the triangular section that is supported or sits above the horizontal structure. It is obvious that there are angels flanking either side of the open Bible and all of the angels are making music of some sort. Some are singing; others are playing the cymbals. According to information I found on their website, there is an indication that the angels originally celebrated the intricacy and beauty of the human form in all its glorious nudity. But, being a church, the decision to put clothes on the angels was made and today they play their music fully clothed.

A close up of the Crescent Hill Baptist Church pediment. Corinthian capitals adorn the tops of the fluted columns.

St. Mark's as seen from across Frankfort Avenue.

ST. MARK'S EPISCOPAL CHURCH

Like the quiet kid brother to a football star, St. Marks stands but a block or two away from Crescent Hill Baptist Church. It is easily overlooked if one drives quickly down Frankfort Avenue, so the large stone cross in the front courtyard really helps to mark its place in the community. Every time I see St. Marks on one corner and the Baptist church on the other, I am reminded of the importance of religion to a community, particularly Southern communities. There is a reason they call it the "Bible Belt" and I have always believed that it is because you really can't swing a dead rat without hitting a church. No matter what your denomination or personal belief system, in Louisville you can pretty well bet that finding a church that will fit your lifestyle is not going to be a Herculean task. If you don't find one on the first corner, go to the next! As a community that prides itself on being a leader in cutting edge theology, Louisville supports many religions and denominations. Yet, even our fair city is has its fair share of irony. Up until about twenty years ago if one walked down Frankfort Avenue, you would first pass the stately old Crescent Hill Library, where you could stop and feed your intellectual appetite. Then, walk a few feet further, and you pass Crescent Hill Baptist, followed by St. Mark's — just in case you felt the need to feed your spiritual hunger. Continue on your walk just one block more — and you could feed whatever instinct was driving you to stop at the only local XXX theatre around! There used to be a large marquee above the theatre that would loudly announce the title and players of whatever movie was running that week. I was a precocious child and I used to love to ride by that place, knowing that it was naughty in some way that a child knows, but doesn't fully understand, and ask loudly of my parents: "Mommy, what does 'Without a Stitch' mean? Watching them look at each other and then quickly look away as they shifted uncomfortably in their seats was the best part of it all and I inwardly snickered when I received an answer like, "It's a medical movie, Honey. Probably someone was injured and they sewed them up without stitches." We all knew it was a lie, but I had to give them credit for thinking quickly on their feet. All of this, both the light and the dark, within about a three block radius! Well, I think back on it and snicker, thinking that perhaps the churches were placed there to act as a deterrent to those who were on their way to the theatre. Or, an alternate scenario is that perhaps the churches were placed there for people who were walking out of the theatre and wanted to repent afterward! What cannot be argued or speculated about, though, is that St. Mark's still stands today much as it did when it was first constructed. A familiar face along Frankfort Avenue the church began as a church school by Mr. Thomas S. Kennedy, the founder of the court that bears his name. The structure reminds one of an old Spanish Mission, as it is simple in form, standing with a solitary bell hanging in the stone bell tower. However, it also puts me in mind of an old Irish church, as a large, stone cross graces the front yard. St. Mark's dates back to the late 1800s and the building that exists today dates to 1895.

THE RECTORY HOUSE

Behind, but not directly behind, St. Mark's church is a house that I have called the "Rectory House" because of the story that the current residents

The original Rectory House of St. Mark's Episcopal Church no longer functions as a rectory. It's now a private residence.

The horizontal panels of stained glass repeat the same design.

Detail of the interior staircase.

passed along to me. I had originally bypassed St. Mark's when I was out researching and taking pictures. I thought that one or two churches would be plenty. Driving down the streets, I noticed a beautiful home that was in the process of renovation and even though it was not finished, it was still quite compelling, so I stopped. Fortune smiled on me that day, for the current residents, a father and daughter, were home. Explaining my interest and my intent, they graciously invited me in and took time from their day to talk to me at length about the house. As I have worked on this book, I have been so pleased to meet and speak with so many people who are willing to help me preserve the beauty and the stories of our city. But, these two individuals, who preferred not to be named,

These stained glass panels are on the right ride of the interior staircase. Reflecting the beauty and elegance of the turn-of-the-century artistry, these panels of rose and yellow illuminate the intricate carvings on the staircase.

went out of their way to give me information and in doing so, became a very real reflection of the kind of Southern hospitality and grace, for which Kentucky is famous. The home, they told me, was once the rectory for St. Mark's and almost everything is original to the home. The structure is very classically Queen Anne, with the candle snuffer turret and large front porch. The homes date to the early nineteen hundreds, which would coordinate nicely with

This stained glass is original to the home and it's amazing that it survived the 1974 tornado. Notice the repeated fleur-de-lis design around the edges of the window. This theme is repeated in other stained glass areas around the home.

the dates of St. Mark's. In addition to the architecture, the stained glass is something that should be noted, as it, too, is original. The 1974 tornado took out one pane of stained glass, but it was replaced nicely and looks original to the home. The pictures included are of the original glass. There is a repeated fleur-de-lis pattern in the windows at the front and also the one on the side. This reflects the importance and pride that the residents took in their city.

The Wood House

The neatest thing about writing this book has been meeting people who are kind enough to share their homes and businesses with me and

The Wood's home as it stands today.

The Wood's home as it looked at the turn of the century.

Portrait of Mr. Wood's relative with the original wallpaper behind it.

who open their lives and their stories quite willingly. The day that I shot pictures of the Wood's home, I had taken off work to be with my little boy, who wasn't feeling well. During the course of the day, as he began to feel better, we decided to take a ride and that I would shoot some pictures while we were out. It was on this excursion that I happened to drive down Kennedy Court and see the perfect example of what I imagined the Queen Anne style to be. When I stopped to ask their permission to put their lovely home in my book, I found that not only were they kind enough to permit me access to their home, but also were quite willing to show me around! I love before and after pictures, and when I spoke to Mr. and Mrs. Woods, the owners of this lovely Queen Anne style home, they were kind enough to let me photograph – and even offered to let me borrow! – a picture of the home as it was when it was originally built in the late 1800s. Again, to say that the people whose homes I have included in this book were gracious would be to make a huge understatement! The Woods have lived in this area for generations and they have lived in the home for many years. While some renovations, again due to the 1974 tornado, were necessary, the turret is original to the structure and the "fish scale" siding to the turret is a reproduction of the original. The interior, which Mr. and Mrs. Woods were kind enough to let me view, has been lovingly furnished with period style pieces, reflecting what it might have looked like originally. The wallpaper, amazingly, has remained in tact and in excellent condition. Original to the home, there was no yellowing or cracking and the beautiful pink and red cabbage rose design added a delicacy to the entry hall. A large picture of Mr. Wood's ancestor hung on the wall and it lent itself to the feel of authenticity of the entire house.

THE FORD HOME

You just never know what you will find when you stop along the way and talk to people, but the Ford home gave a very interesting story to go with the pictures. All homes on Kennedy Avenue are elegant Victorian homes, but Ms. Ford informed me that at the center of the Kennedy Court once stood the Kennedy mansion. It was a large family home, and it is unfortunate that my research did not uncover more information about it. However, when Mr. Kennedy's daughters married and began families of their own, he had two houses built for them, one on one side of his and

Stained glass from the Ford home.

The Ford home as seen from the opposite side of the street.

this one on the other. It reminded me of the story of the Wesley House and it must have been very common for affluent families to stay in close proximity to each other, and, as one elderly resident noted, everything that one could possibly want or need was in walking distance. There was really no reason to look or go anywhere else.

The Ford Home is a small version of Queen Anne, which is a term that refers to many different styles of Victorian home. The stained glass is original to the home, and if one looks closely, there is a resemblance to the stained glass of the Wesley House. The sharp gables and the wrap-around front porch make this home look like it might have originally been part of the set of "Our Town."

The Merriwether House sits atop a great, green hill that overlooks Harrod's Creek. Built to resemble a boat, one can make out what the architect hoped would resemble a wheel house at the top of the home.

Detailed in the overhang on the porch is a star or "Mariner's Compass" design. This further reinforces the nautical theme that Mary Merriwether established in the architecture of the home.

Chapter Six:
HISTORIC ETCETERAS

There is not always a category where we can put something that we really enjoy, but yet we like it too much to leave it out. That is the way I feel about the buildings in this portion of the book. While they do not fit into any specific category or district, they are a hodgepodge of all kinds of neat artistic styles and architectural creativity. I would be doing a great disservice to those who want to sample the architecture of our city if I left out these places that mean so much to me. Each one tells a different story or has a special significance to it and spending a little time getting to know these places sheds light on many historical issues and puts the past into perspective.

One of the things I have always enjoyed was a drive down River Road. It's a winding two lane pathway that leads straight into the heart of downtown Louisville, yet lets you stop off in Butchertown and several other places along the way. In the early morning light you can see the skyline of the city and the Aegon Building towering above all the rest. The Humana Building glows green these days and the bridges create a picturesque backdrop for the river itself. I have been driving that road for years and had always been intrigued by a home that set back from the road, recessed on its own little pathway. An historic marker was placed in the front yard, but I had never stopped to look at it or read what was on it. The house sits right on Harrod's Creek, which was named for Captain James Harrod, who in the late 1700s founded Fort Harrod, which is known today as Harrodsburg. In front of the house, the Merriwether House, is a one-lane bridge through which cars have been negotiating passage since my mother was a child. As I sat on one side, waiting for a stream of cars to pass so that I could take my turn, I decided to stop and read the marker for the home. While I had read the words "Meriwether House," I had always assumed that it had some connection to Meriwether Lewis of the Lewis and Clark exploration. After all, Locust Grove, a stopping point for the two explorers, was just around the corner. What unfolded before me, however, was a treasure trove of information that I had no idea even existed.

It is known as the "Meriwether House" and I had the good fortune to speak to one of the grandnieces of Harry and Isaac Merriwether. A student at Ballard High School, Ms. Merriwether was kind enough to give me information that can only come from a family member who have treasured the stories of its ancestors and continue to pass them along from generation to generation, like a precious heirloom. The land, 1.5 acres, had been bought from the Allison family in 1891 for about $55. She informed me that the property was, at one time, a retirement home for former slaves. It had also been a stopping place for tourists and travelers through the years. Harry and Isaac Merriwether were the first African American landowners in the area. I noted that it was very interesting that in 1891, they were able to buy the land from a white family. I wondered aloud to Ms. Merriwether

Even the windows remind you of portholes, a clever addition to this interesting home.

if this was not a commentary on the progressive nature of Louisville and how strong the roots of abolition had been. Of course, this is conjecture and since the families never revealed the details of the property transfer, history remains silent on the incident. The property had remained in her family for six generations, however, and most of the ornamentation to the structure is original to the home. She stated that the house used to have a winding front porch that wrapped around the home. However, half of the original porch had been removed. She also noted that the home's architecture had been constructed so that the home resembled a boat or ship. It had never occurred to me that the exact reason that the house had caught my interest was that it looked like something…but I could not pin down exactly what it resembled. Not adhering to any particular structural code or style, the house was just *different*, but not so much so that one could not tell that it was built in the mid to late 1800s. While it lacks the gingerbread motif of the classical Victorian homes of the day, the cutout Mariner's Compass design in the overhang or awning of the front porch would tip one off that this was nautically designed but still Victorian. If viewed from the front, one can almost make out the wheelhouse at the very top. Knowing the history of Harrod's Creek, it is not far-fetched that the brothers would have chosen such a clever design for the home. Harrod's Creek was a stopping place for flatboats and their crews. As it is one of two creeks bordered by the Ohio River on one side and lush green hills on the other, it became an area that was very popular for the affluent of the age. Yet, throughout the years and despite changes in the city, the Merriwether House has remained unchanged itself.

THE INN AT WOODHAVEN

Beds and Breakfasts are usually charming and grace any neighborhood with their presence, as they exude gentility and hospitality from every corner. At least, if every bed and breakfast were modeled after the Inn at Woodhaven, this would be the case. Nestled into a little nook that one might just pass by, unless specifically looking for the home, the Inn sits in the heart of Saint Matthews, an east end district known for refinement and luxury. From a distance it looks quite like a quaint little gingerbread house, beckoning its guests to come and sit for a while while sharing the goodies within. My husband and I had the good fortune of spending the night at the Inn at Woodhaven, so I can personally vouch that the complimentary chocolate covered strawberries, miniature pecan pies, and the tea basket prepared by Ms. Burton and her helpers were some of the most delicious delicacies we have had in a long, long time. The Inn at Woodhaven is dedicated to making guests, both those who travel from out of town and those of us who just want to get away from the hustle and bustle of the inner city, feel as if they have their own private getaway where the world is kept at bay — at least for the night. In the midst of an area that prides itself on its malls and shopping centers, the Inn at Woodhaven offers a quiet respite from noise that exists outside of its parameters. As I pulled into the driveway to take pictures, Ms. Marsha Burton, current owner and Innkeeper, was busy preparing for her guests. Yet, as I expected, the elegance of the home was only rivaled by the graciousness of the owner and she was more than happy to give me all the juicy tidbits that she could. Ms. Burton stated that the establishment had once housed the twenty children of

The white Adirondack chairs in front of the Inn at Woodhaven beckon guests to come and "sit a spell."

The Rose Cottage is nestled off to the side of the main home and is a wonderful place to spend a honeymoon night. Ms. Burton states that the Rose Cottage is in use almost every day of the year. It certainly isn't hard to see why!

the original owners and we mused about how one could imagine the children swinging on the limbs of the grand old tree that still stands in the front yard. Interestingly, all twenty children survived to adulthood, an almost unheard of feat for the mid-1800s. They were the children of Theodore Brown, a local farmer who was interested in architecture and whose letters on the subject of architecture and design reside in the Smithsonian Institution in Washington D.C. She stated that the Inn was once called "Woodview" and that it sat on approximately five hundred acres of land that Brown inherited from his father. The architect, A. J. Downing, was a prominent designer of the age and instead of designing an opulent villa for Mr. Brown, he instead gave him a very respectable, middle class residence for that day and age. Characterized as "Gothic Revival," the home was built in 1853 and boasts two and a half stories of yellow brick house, trimmed in white gingerbread. The carriage house in back is one of the few original carriages houses in Louisville

The back of the Inn at Woodhaven.

The Carriage House still stands much as it did originally, except without the horses or carriages! Renovations to the interior make it a wonderful place to spend a night or two.

that's still intact. The cupola on top of the carriage house is also original to the building, which is amazing given the fact that many were torn off during the 1974 tornado. A new addition to the home was the octagon shaped Rose Cottage, which is located on the side of the house and was built in 1998. The amount of detail that went into making certain that the Rose Cottage was architecturally identical and true to the original plans that Mr. Downing had for the home won the Rose Cottage the 1998 Homebuilders Association Award. Both the main and carriage house have been awarded several restoration awards and the home is located on the National Register of Historic Places.

HISTORIC LOCUST GROVE

Discovering Locust Grove is like unpacking your grandmother's cedar trunk or hope chest, only to find that she had buried an heirloom underneath the dresses, hats, and pictures of the past. Locust Grove is a site that people in Louisville often hear about and school children may take a field trip there, but other than that, it's just a place that locals never really take the time to explore in depth. As I stood at the entrance to the gift shop, I watched as a family took pictures of the statue of General George Rogers Clark, which stands outside the entry like a sentinel protecting the former home and grounds. "I can't believe I have lived here my entire life and never knew this place existed," one woman remarked to her companions. "What a gift this is!" I knew exactly what she meant. The first time I ever set foot on the historic grounds was in 2005 and after seeing it, I could not believe it

The gardens of Locust Grove are legendary and every year there is a peddler's market and garden fair on the grounds of the estate.

took me thirty-five years to actually appreciate it! Knowing the importance of George Rogers Clark and the contributions he made to the founding and settling of Louisville makes Locust Grove an interesting landmark. However, it sweetens the archaeological and historical pot to know that William Clark and Meriwether Lewis often made Locust Grove a stopping point on their travels. We know for a fact that after they reached the Pacific Coast, they stopped by Locust Grove on their way back to have a welcome home celebration. The Lewis and Clark exploration, also known as the Corps of Discovery, had been commissioned by Thomas Jefferson in 1803 to explore the Northwest Territory and journal about the plant

The front of the home as seen from the road.

Locust Grove is a study in simple Georgian/Federal style symmetry and balance.

Even the garden path that leads to a small shed-like house is balanced and symmetrical.

and animal life they found along the way. They were to keep records and report their findings. They also collected specimens along the way and one of these, a horn from a big horn sheep, is the only known animal artifact remaining from the exploration. In addition to Lewis and Clark, the Corps was made up of Sacagawea, their Native American guide, York, Clark's slave, and nine men from Kentucky. Starting out from the Falls of the Ohio on October 26, 1803, they were not sure what they would find, but they were determined that they would not return empty handed. The information they brought back with them set a course for the "Manifest Destiny" of our country. Locust Grove is tied to this historical group by the kinship of William Clark to his eldest brother, George Rogers

Locust Grove.

Clark, who had gone to live with their younger sister, Lucy Clark Croghan. Lucy had married Major William Croghan, establishing Locust Grove as a family residence. The couple had met and fallen in love, much to the chagrin of the Clark family who had hoped for a better social match for Lucy than William Croghan. Yet, as young

An outbuilding on Locust Grove.

people in love often do, they held their ground and married on July 14, 1789. It was an interesting date for their marriage, in retrospect, since it was the exact date of the storming of the Bastille in France, marking the beginning of the French Revolution. As volatile as situations were in other parts of the world, the life of the Croghans was relatively easy, with Lucy partnering with her husband in the running of the home and the family surveying business. They were married for thirty-four years, rearing eight children. General George Rogers Clark came to live with the Croghans after he had his right leg amputated and had suffered a stroke. Locust Grove remained a home of hospitality and generosity, and now stands as a testament to the spirit of those who founded our country and in particular, our state. Locust Grove was founded in 1790 and the architectural style is classified as "Georgian," which was popular in the colonies and in England in the late 1700s to around 1840. The name derives from George's of the British monarchy and the distinguishing characteristics would be the regularity of form and the simplicity of the front of the home or building. There was a great emphasis on the fronts of the homes all having a very similar look to them, so it is not surprising that strict adherence to symmetry is one of the most important aspects. The windows were usually precisely balanced in their length and width and the trim and cornices is often painted white, which contrasts to the red or tan walls. Brick is a very popular material to use in Georgian styled buildings, however, it is not unusual to find wooden, timber framed, or plank homes in this style, as well. The Georgian style, known sometimes as "Federal," is common for the time period, as many settlers still held great pride in their European roots and reflected this in the styling and furnishing of their homes.

The Zachary Taylor house as seen from the front.

ZACHARY TAYLOR HOUSE

Driving down U.S. Highway 42, you cannot mistake the military cemetery that bears the name of our twelfth president. The rock wall that surrounds it only piques the interest of the passerby and you will find yourself peeking in as you crest the hill or pass the entrance of the Zachary Taylor Cemetery. The endless lines of identical grave markers reminds me of the nameless, faceless men who fought, and died, for my personal freedom. While my family was not one who had a very strong military background, I have one great-grandfather, Norman Rudolph, who is buried in the Zachary Taylor Cemetery. He had fought in World War I and I remember my grandmother telling the story of how he had died of "shell shock." That was the only term my family knew, since education about PTSD (Post Traumatic Stress Disorder) is a fairly new thing. Stories were told about "Poppy" and what a good man he was. But, as happens to almost every single person who sees the horrors and ravages of war, he came back from Europe a changed man. Unable to live a normal life with his wife and two small daughters, he lived the remainder of his days in the VA Hospital until his death. The Zachary Taylor Cemetery was named for the President who was born in Virginia, but claimed Kentucky as his home. Nicknamed "Old Rough and Ready" because of his unusually disheveled appearance, Taylor endeared himself to those around him because of his lack of pretension. Distinguishing himself as a formidable military leader in the Mexican-American War, he was elected president in 1849 and then promptly died in 1850. There are several interesting facts about Taylor, the most unusual being the mystery that surrounded his death. While the history books report that Taylor died of gastroenteritis, a very painful abdominal condition, many historians believe that there was a conspiracy to cover up the fact that Taylor was assassinated – namely poisoned – while in office. There had always been speculation that Taylor had been given arsenic, which was relatively untraceable in the mid 1800s, but until there were tests to determine this, history had to wait for technology to catch up. Since Taylor is buried in the cemetery that bears his name, in 1991 his relatives gave permission to the coroner's office to exhume his body and lay the mystery of the his death to rest, once and for all. Upon testing the body for levels of arsenic, the coroner's findings were consistent with the belief that the President had died of natural causes and not arsenic poisoning. There were levels of arsenic present, but since all decomposing bodies have small amounts of it, there was not enough to state that arsenic might have been a cause of the President's demise. The coroner stated that if arsenic poisoning had been a probable cause for his death, the levels would have been much higher than what they found. However, a very likely cause, historians say, was that the President died of multiple organ failure due to a severe heat stroke that he suffered at the dedication of the Washington Monument. His complaints and symptoms do appear to be consistent with that theory. As for the Zachary Taylor House, you really have to be looking for it to find it. Unlike Locust Grove, it does not sit directly out on the street where one could just run into it inadvertently. While it is close in proximity to Locust Grove, it sits back on a quiet little street, off the beaten path. As I was shooting pictures of Locust Grove, I drove past the historic marker twice before I actually stopped and looked for the house. Like most treasures, happening upon them unexpectedly and then being pleasantly surprised is the best part of it. As I am always a little sheepish about approaching complete strangers about their beautiful or unusual dwellings, I was very relieved at the graciousness of Mrs. Barbara Gist, who invited me to take as many pictures as I liked. Additionally, she and her husband, Dr. William Gist, gave me information about the home and a recent article published about the home. The home, named Springfield, was the boyhood home of Zachary Taylor. His father, Colonel Richard Taylor, had moved to the 400-acre Kentucky plot of land from Virginia when Zachary was an infant. The land grew and the Taylors became as prosperous a family in Kentucky as they ever had been in Virginia. The estimated amount of property on one record indicated that they owned approximately 10,000 acres of land at one time. Zachary lived at Springfield until he was about twenty-one years of age. The bricks that make up the large Georgian manor house were actually fired on the site. The house was constructed somewhere around 1785-1790, but the home that is standing now was not the original home of the Taylors. Like most young families, they started out in a more modest home. The original home was a log cabin, but that was moved to the back of the property and eventually used as slave quarters. Zachary's military career took him all over the country, but he always returned to Springfield, where he and his wife raised their children. All but one, Sarah Knox, was born in the house. And, ironically, Sarah's place in the annals of Kentucky

The home as seen from the back. It's not hard to imagine a very young Sarah Taylor sipping lemonade and being courted by a handsome Jefferson Davis on the porch of the lovely home.

history is more interesting than any of the other siblings who were born there! Sarah Knox Taylor was a beautiful young girl who had fallen in love with a handsome, young military officer by the name of Jefferson Davis. They desperately wanted to be married, but Taylor would not allow it, as he did not want to see his beautiful young daughter married to a soldier. So, knowing that there was only one way for him to be granted the hand of the woman he loved, Davis resigned from the army and married Taylor's daughter. Both became ill shortly after the marriage, contracting malaria according to the historic reports. Davis survived, but, sadly, Sarah died three months after their marriage. It was rumored that Taylor never forgave Davis and blamed him for the death of his daughter. Davis left and went on some years later to re-marry. If the name Jefferson Davis does not sound familiar to you, it might be that Civil War history is not in the forefront of your mind. While almost everyone knows about Abraham Lincoln, his log cabin, his rail splitting days, and how he was from Kentucky, very few people know that the Civil War was the only time in history where we as a nation had two Presidents fighting for two different sides, both of whom had been born in Kentucky. Abraham Lincoln was President of the Union and fought to preserve it and abolish slavery while Jefferson Davis, also born in Kentucky, was President of the Confederacy and fought for the seceding states. The Zachary Taylor House, also known as Springfield, will one day become a museum, the Gists hope, and their careful preservation of this historic landmark should ensure that people will get to enjoy it for generations to come.

CHURCHILL DOWNS

You didn't think we had heard the last about our good friend William Clark and the Clark family, now did you? After telling you how involved the Clarks were in the history of Kentucky and how important they were to the founding of the city, you must know by now that the younger generations will often take over for the older ones. Sometimes this is a good thing — and sometimes it is a bad thing. There begins that sad case of Lutie Clark and how it is that Churchill Downs once led a man to his downfall and then his demise, by suicide.

General William Clark, who is mentioned previously in this book, had a son. This son married a lady from a very prominent local family. Her name was Abigail Prather Churchill. They had a son whom they named Meriwether Lewis Clark, Jr. in honor of the great men and their exploration. This child, nicknamed "Lutie" by his mother, knew privilege and wealth, but would not be able to attain happiness, it seems. The Clarks had long been avid equine aficionados, leaving behind papers that record the names, dates of birth, and very detailed descriptions of the many foals they owned. It would appear that the link to the future of Churchill Downs was inextricably linked to that age-old belief in pedigree and birth right. Just as the horses were recorded and prized for their bloodlines and performance, so too were the children born to prominent families of that day and age. Marriages to other families of similar class and status and the births of subsequent generations were recorded and prized for their unions. It was a time where class and pedigree was everything—whether you were a horse or a person.

The pedigree of Lutie Clark was obvious. However, it was really the link to the Churchills that gave him the tie to the Downs and the Derby. Lutie's mother died when he was a small boy and he was sent to live with his maternal aunt and her two brothers, John and Henry Churchill. They, too, were lovers of horses and racing, so Lutie came by his passion for the sport naturally. His interest

waned through the years and it was only after some gentlemen approached him about taking an interest in the decline of the sport in Louisville, that his interest was renewed. He took a year and went to Europe to study their betting systems and how they made money on the sport. He came back invigorated and with new ideas about how to renew the public's interest in this, the sport of kings. He paid special attention to the betting systems of Paris, called Parimutuel betting. It was a system where all the bets were placed in a pool, the house would take their share off the top, and the odds would be calculated on the remainder of the bets. For a non-mathematical person such as myself, the algebraic equation that explains this system made no sense whatsoever. However, it did seem to work for the Parisians, who were prospering from the system. Lutie returned with his new information and a plan. Along with local investors and the backing from the Churchill family, the racetrack was born. Through the years, Lutie developed a very bad reputation as being a bit hot-headed and unstable. Pulling guns on men who had insulted him, and actually being shot once himself because of his insulting tongue, made him a poor bet when it came to dividing up the three hundred acres of land that the Churchills owned. When his uncle Henry died, he left the entirety of his estate to his wife and their children. When his uncle John died, he left everything to his wife and heirs, minus forty-six acres that would go to Lutie. It was a mere pittance compared to what the others received, but it also stipulated that Lutie was to have no controlling interest or association with the racetrack itself. He acted as a steward there for many years. His temper grew worse and, very likely, his feelings of being left out did not help that. The place where he worked began to gain the nickname "Churchill's downs" in some part referring to the downfall of the man with the great name and pedigree. After losing money through the years, specifically in the Stock Market, Lutie finally ended it all when he took his own life. He committed suicide in 1899. His contribution to Kentucky history and the culture of Louisville cannot be omitted nor overlooked. He began what would come to be known worldwide as the greatest two minutes in sports and for that, our city remembers him and we are grateful for his contribution.

The year 1875 is considered the year of the first running of the Kentucky Derby. Those of us who grew up in Louisville or the surrounding area know what a huge deal this one day really is. Celebrities from all over the world crowd into Millionaires Row and grace our city with their presence and prestige. It is an exciting day that we in Louisville prepare for starting in April with the Kentucky Derby Festival. It is our answer to Mardi Gras and is a time when people line the streets showing off hot-rod cars and others go to the Fillie Ball or myriad other black-tie affairs. There is a Chow Wagon, where you can get a steaming, hot bowl of Kentucky Burgoo or other fair styled cuisine. Live music and bands play along the river and there is always the Derby Parade. It all leads up to the first Saturday in May and those of us who do not wish to brave the crowds, usually stay home and barbeque with friends and family. Everyone settles down around 6 p.m. as the most exciting race of the day begins. The "Call to the Post" is heard, trumpeting over the din of the drunks in the infield and the elegant folks in the grandstands. Whenever this is heard, the playing of "My Old Kentucky Home" cannot be far behind. Fortunately, the words of the song have been changed over the years so that the former lyrics, which included racial epithets, are no longer sung out to thousands of tourists. Still, the tune is familiar and everyone, Kentuckian and Non-Kentuckian alike, do their best to remember the words that the bourbon and mint have dimmed slightly. The ladies in their glorious hats and the gentlemen in their suits and ties all begin to scream like little children as their horse breaks from the starting gate and in just two minutes, the new winner makes his way toward the finish line. It is indeed exciting. The winning horse is given a garland of roses, which is an exquisite sight to behold. The making of the garland is an event that takes from ten to twelve hours and is open to the public. Each garland holds 564 roses, and not just any roses, mind you. Out of every rose bush, there is only one prime rose. It is the best of the best and this means that every garland of roses needs 564 rose bushes so that one rose may be chosen. On the garland, there is a crown of roses with one rose for each horse that runs in the Derby race. In that crown, there will be one rose that stands a little higher than the rest, symbolizing the strength of heart of the winner, the one who stands as better than the rest. There is also a handsome purse that goes along with being the winner and a nice trophy, but the greatest gift that Churchill Downs gives to the city is the history and legacy pride in our community that we are able to pass down to future generations.

FINAL THOUGHTS

I hope that you have enjoyed a look at the sprinkling of homes and businesses that I have included here. Louisville is a city rich in history and culture and I have thoroughly enjoyed researching the structures and meeting the people who love this city and its historic buildings as much as I do. So the next time you are in town, take a day to visit some of the places listed here. You might be surprised at just how you will grow to love the people, the places, and the architecture of Louisville.

Blooms abound at Churchill Downs even in the summer. It is a place that is well known for its gorgeous display of tulips in the spring.

FOOTNOTES

http://www.afn.org/~afn03098/cppaper.htm

http://freenet.buffalo.edu/bah/a/archsty/rom/index.html#rr

Becker, Fred. www.fredbecker.org/News%20Letter/Q%20Anne%20Arch.htm

http://en.wikipedia.org/wiki/Modern_architecture

Leland, Michael. http://www.michael.leleand.name/postmodern/index.html

Kennedy, Albert Joseph and Woods, Robert Archy. Charities Publication Committee, 1911.

Hampton, Roy. 1896. (No publisher or city – web archive)

Winifred, Sister Mary. http://www.ourladychurch.net/history/OurLadyHistory_Chapter_1937_Flood.htm

http://www.marinehospital.org/past.htm

Barrett, Sheila. "Big Jim Porter, The Kentucky Giant." http://sheilabarrett.wordpress.com/category/big-jim-porter/